YOU ARE YOUR HEALER

YOU ARE YOUR HEALER

The Ultimate Guide to Heal Your Past,
Transform Your Life
& Awaken to Your True Self

YOL SWAN

Sri Devi Press
Asheville

Publisher's Note

This publication is sold with the understanding that neither the publisher nor the author is engaged in rendering psychological, medical, legal, or other professional services. If expert assistance is needed, a certified professional should be sought.

Copyright © 2022 by Yol Swan
Sri Devi Press
P.O. Box 2033
Asheville, NC 28802
All rights reserved. No part of this publication may be reproduced, distributed, or transmitted in any form or by any means without the prior written permission of the publisher.

Cataloging-in-Publication Data

Name: Swan, Yol, author.
Title: You are your healer : the ultimate guide to heal your past, transform your life & awaken to your true self / Yol Swan.
Description: Asheville : Sri Devi Press, [2022] | Includes bibliographical references.
Identifiers: ISBN: 978-0-9863654-5-4 (paperback) | 978-0-9863654-6-1 (hardcover) | 978-0-9863654-4-7 (ebook/kindle) | LCCN: 2022911239
Subjects: LCSH: Self-actualization (Psychology) | Self-consciousness (Awareness) | Self-realization. | Change (Psychology) | Becoming (Philosophy) | Mind and body. | Self-care, Health. | Spiritual healing. | Happiness. | Peace of mind. | Spiritual life. | BISAC: SELF-HELP / Spiritual. | SELF-HELP / Personal Growth / Happiness. | BODY, MIND & SPIRIT / Healing / Prayer & Spiritual. | BODY, MIND & SPIRIT / Mindfulness & Meditation.
Classification: LCC: BF637.S4 S93 2022 | DDC: 158.1--dc23

Also by Yol Swan

The Indigo Journals
Spiritual Healing For Indigo Adults & Other Feminine Souls

Songs of Light and Dark
Poetic Meditations on the Self & Random Haikus

YolSwan.com

The Realized Being sees only the Self, just as the goldsmith sees only the gold while valuing it in various jewels made of gold. When you identify yourself with the body, name and form are there. But when you transcend the body-consciousness, the "others" also disappear. The Realized One does not see the world as different from himself.

— *Ramana Maharshi*

Table of Contents

Introduction	xi
THE PREMISE: ONENESS	
1. The Paradoxical Essence of Consciousness	3
Developing Stillness	20
2. The Complex Nature of Your Soul	23
The Gross Body	27
The Subtle Body	29
The Causal Body	38
Soham-Hamsa Pranayama	43
THE REVELATION: A DIVINE PLAY	
3. The Karmic Unfolding of Reality	47
The Love-Consciousness Pyramid	61
Basic Steps to Reduce Negative Karma	74
4. A Spiritual View of Ego	79
The Best Version of You	101

THE PROCESS:
INDIVIDUATION IN DUALITY

5. Your Egoic Sense of Otherness	107
Radical Honesty Process	127
6. The Mental Movie You Call Your Life	135
Retrieving Your Little Orphans	149

THE SWAN METHOD:
FROM OTHERNESS TO SELF

7. Reclaiming Your Inner Power	155
Anchoring in the Consciousness "I Am"	178
8. Healing the Past Through the Present	181
Main Guidelines	195

THE GOAL: SPIRITUAL FREEDOM

9. Awakening to Your True Self	211
Living in Pure Awareness	233
Glossary	245
About the Author	253

Introduction

What would your life feel like if you could let go of the past to be completely present and at peace in the moment? What if you had a method to do this on an ongoing basis, to heal a wounded perception that hampers your full spiritual potential? This book will show you how. It is the result of more than thirty years exploring the mind, psychology, and spirituality, as well as my own process of self-discovery, mystical experiences, and professional work helping clients around the world gain emotional and spiritual freedom.

It is not about being a healer in the traditional sense but about healing yourself by realizing that you have everything you need to experience happiness and peace, because your original, divine nature is happiness and peace. It is for you if you are a spiritual seeker ready to delve deeply within to leave the past behind and remove the painful limitations of your mind. Now, it is not about manifesting all your desires or attracting everything you want, which seem to be prevailing themes these days. On the contrary, it will help you see why there is no real fulfillment in such external pursuits, only more bondage leading to suffering.

I will guide you to unravel the codependent patterns that enslave you to all kinds of illusions and expectations, keeping you in a polarizing delusion of duality that causes dissatisfaction and pain. I will show you a path toward emotional and spiritual freedom, but what you gain from this book will depend on where you are on your journey and how much you are willing to invest in your own liberation. If you are a sincere seeker, it can completely transform your perception and experience of life by revealing the paradoxical forces that shape your reality, while helping you peel away what blocks your divinity. You don't have to control or fix anything, but you must take full responsibility to clear your path.

My own spiritual adventure started in my late twenties, after difficult relationships with family, partners, and friends had led me to several years of psychoanalysis. At some point during this process, I felt compelled to cut off from the world almost completely, to go further within, in the hopes of getting to the root of my discontent. Unexpected circumstances allowed me to do this for almost four years without worrying about financial or social responsibilities, so I immersed myself in a continuous self-exploration while focusing on various creative projects. Little did I know this would bring about a spiritual awakening and launch me into a lifelong quest for Divine Consciousness!

You see, I had rejected anything that even smelled like religion from a very early age, arguing with my mother to avoid going to Sunday school as a child. In spite of her Catholic faith and family expectations, she was an intellectual woman liberal enough to spare me any traditional rituals. My father was a staunch atheist, angry at God and the world, so he didn't care either way. To me, God was portrayed as an authority figure I couldn't accept, but I perceived life as energy and always felt guided from within. I had no understanding of any of this until this "personal retreat" completely changed me. There are no words to describe my experience. All I can say is that the Divine cracked me open like a nut to reveal itself as the eternal Presence pervading life—in me and all around me. Nothing ever felt more real than that, and my resistance to God immediately vanished.

A subtler doorway into myself spontaneously opened, leading to memories of past lives, for which I had no conceptual background, since all of this was new to me. A veil was pulled away, giving me access to higher dimensions of existence and prodding me to accept my highly sensitive and intuitive nature, which I had always seen as a burden. I began observing how my reality reflected what I was processing and discovering in myself, which would come to be a fundamental aspect of my spiritual work later in life. Being in solitude also made clear that my unhappiness had nothing to do with anyone or anything external; it was the result of my own perception and choices, both past and present, crystallizing as my reality and coloring—or rather, distorting—my experience of life.

I began meditating without intending to, or even knowing what I was doing, which eventually turned into a more disciplined, daily practice of sitting still. I got a few books on Buddhism and Taoism, hoping to get some direction and a better understanding of the mystical realms in which I often found myself. I didn't actualize those teachings until a few years later, when I was drawn to a forty-day Vipassana retreat with an enlightened Theravada master from Thailand, who initiated me as a nun.

With shaved head and eyebrows, dressed in a simple white robe, I followed a very austere, mindful lifestyle that quickly transformed Buddha's teachings from mere concepts into real experiences. I began to comprehend the nature of the mind, as well as how to silence it, which allowed me to get a taste of the superconsciousness state known as *nirvana*. However, the Buddhist path proved a bit too austere and hard on my body, so I left it behind once I moved to the United States to study music, where I was guided to a few liberated gurus who initiated me into their Vedic traditions and practices.

Life blessed me with the presence of several saints, trips to Thailand and India, and a wealth of retreats and transcendental states. On one occasion, while in India, at the ashram of one of my teachers, I spontaneously experienced a full awakening. It was not a trancelike, superconscious state (such as *samadhi* or *nirvana*), which I had had in deep meditation, where I would go out completely and come back feeling clearer and renewed. This happened while I was in the kitchen putting my dishes away, as I did every day. An intense force suddenly took over me, and I became Pure Awareness, One-With-All, watching life from a plane of no-mind, of complete inner silence and peace. It is not possible to describe this, for everything looked the same but my *experience* of it was absolutely different. The usual sense of separation from people and objects was gone, there was no self-consciousness or self-centeredness, and the world didn't have its familiar, painful density!

It wasn't a permanent state, and falling back into ordinary consciousness proved to be the most excruciating moment of my life. I felt so trapped by the mind and physical body that I wanted to die. In a harrowing contrast with the complete spiritual freedom I had just tasted, this felt as if my soul was being squished into a constrictive container of suffering. I cried and cried from a fathomless despair until I couldn't cry anymore, out of exhaustion. This event left a deep imprint and fueled the de-

Introduction

sire to find the way back to that purity of being. It also made clear that this feeling of entrapment, separation, and loss is the constant suffering of the human condition underlying every experience—what we all try to escape or buffer with all sorts of distractions, addictions, and fleeting moments of pleasure.

In time, after many years of spiritual transmissions, techniques, insights, visions, and profound states of dispassion and bliss—as well as the joys and struggles of family, social and spiritual groups, marriage, motherhood, divorce, and personal rebirth—I felt increasingly drawn toward solitude and silence again. My internal process, spiritual practices, and studies in yoga philosophy finally led me to the non-dual path of Self-knowledge or spiritual wisdom (*jnana yoga*) and the practice of self-inquiry. This book aims to take you on a similar path, from a dual to a non-dual perception of life.

You will learn the Swan Method, a personal healing system that congealed as a result of the knowledge acquired throughout the years; it empowered me to turn my life around after a series of painful events. Having all the rugs pulled from under me forced me to further investigate the nature of reality. I have integrated ancient philosophical teachings with some of the tools I have learned or developed over more than thirty years through my self-exploration, spiritual practices, and working with clients from all walks of life. Since I use the yoga and Advaita Vedanta philosophical schools as the foundation to explore the mind and the path to enlightenment, I have included informal transliterations of Sanskrit terms to clarify certain concepts, which can also be found in the Glossary.

I consider this ancient wisdom essential to frame a truly transformative process, but I also offer practical, step-by-step instructions to unravel the mental patterns that distort your self-perception and experience of life. This requires a clear view of the ego-mind, which is the source of your suffering, and therefore the central focus of the book. I have distilled perennial knowledge into an ongoing method to remove the sense of separation the ego creates, using the more complex, paradoxical notions around it as guidelines for self-knowledge. However, as you learn to turn the mind inward to know yourself, all these mental concepts lose their usefulness and should be dropped to transcend the mind. They are like a boat you rely on to cross a river but that you no longer need to carry once you get to the other side.

I will take you through an internal process to recognize what makes your journey difficult and what you are here to learn, so you may navigate life more gracefully toward your final destination: the mystical re-union or *yoga* with your true Self (God) that is beyond time, space, and sensory perception. As you cultivate self-awareness to leave the past behind, you will be able to relinquish your unconscious attachment to pain arising from false, yet deeply ingrained beliefs about yourself, as well as the negative dynamics inherent in your ego-mind.

The clearest expression of the Divine is inner peace. It has nothing to do with religion, for it is your essence, emerging spontaneously as you clear a perception tainted with illusions, fears, and unconscious guilt. It prevails behind your mental-emotional fluctuations as the backdrop of all your experiences. At some point, your suffering compels you to seek something more permanent and real to hold on to, until you are able to remove the delusions that obstruct your true nature. You cannot force this process, for it unfolds on its own as you clear your

Introduction

mind of ego. Reject any ideas of where you think you *should* be and start where you are. I encourage you to remain open as you move forward, to uncover deeper aspects of yourself and new possibilities of being.

This guide will help you release the past and dissolve the false identifications distorting your experience of reality. Once you recognize the illusion of *otherness* through which you continuously perceive and judge yourself, you begin to break free from the patterns of codependency and deception produced by your ego that keep you stuck in the past. If you follow the Swan Method with discipline and continuity, your life will become the journey of self-discovery it is meant to be, rather than something to control or fix. In turn, this will effect a real transformation, liberating you from the bondage of your limiting beliefs and mental fluctuations.

I think it is important to read this book in order, to assimilate its concepts and practice the exercises provided; they have been carefully chosen to help you implement the Swan Method on a daily basis and develop increasing self-awareness. They are simple but also meant to diminish the aspects of the mind hampering real growth. This multilayered, integrative approach will help you dissolve the imaginary differences between you, others, and the Divine, which are the real cause of your sorrow. I have used it to rebuild my life after emotional, legal, financial, and physical struggles, experiencing greater peace and many miracles along the way, as well as a much clearer spiritual direction.

Concepts alone will not take you far unless you actualize them in your reality, so practice and repetition are essential! As you will learn shortly, the ego is very elusive; it hides behind your identifications to prevent you from knowing yourself. But it loses its grip as you delve within in search of the truth, eventually disappearing in the immensity of the eternal Self you really are.

I have organized the process in five main sections:

1. In THE PREMISE: ONENESS, I explore the paradoxical essence of Divine Consciousness dreaming a cosmic dream and appearing in a great multiplicity of forms through the elements and qualities of nature. I describe the nature of the soul as an individualized spark of Consciousness wrapped in energy layers, transmigrating from one physical body to another. These are the vehicles through which the Supreme Self experiences itself through its human appearances while innately drawing them to seek liberation from all experience.

2. In THE REVELATION: A DIVINE PLAY, I explain how past actions determine the unfolding of both individual and collective reality; how the various elements of the psyche shape it; and how your experience of it results from your perception, which is invariably tainted with past impressions and the issues and desires your soul reincarnates to resolve. I compare this individual journey to climbing a Love-Consciousness Pyramid and explore the shape-shifting and revolving quality of the ego-mind that brings you to the lower, painful levels of the Pyramid by controlling your mental-emotional states and behavior.

3. In THE PROCESS: INDIVIDUATION IN DUALITY, I delve more deeply into the elusive nature of the ego and its projection as the external world through what I call your *sense of otherness*, the main aspect that maintains the delusion of

duality, separation, and opposition causing power dynamics and pain. I describe its various stages of development in your perception and how it gets reflected in your life, which is a personal projection (or movie) of past karma, impressions, and desires in need of resolution.

4. In THE SWAN METHOD: FROM OTHERNESS TO SELF, I shed light onto the codependent patterns and power dynamics of ego that trap you in the past—in a wounded child archetype—thus preventing you from embracing life as it is, fully present in the moment. I take you step by step through my Method to heal the past by exploring the present to uncover the true meaning behind the situations you encounter. I show you how to pierce through the illusion of *otherness* that holds you back by disrupting your individuation and growth, as you develop dispassion and reclaim the power to redirect the mind toward your Inner Self.

5. Finally, in THE GOAL: SPIRITUAL FREEDOM, I help you take your process of self-exploration even further by dropping all the labels and concepts that keep you in the ordinary ego consciousness that creates suffering, so that you may break free from your own mental entrapment. By embracing life as a mirror and investigating the ego-mind through self-awareness and self-inquiry, you will gradually dissolve your false identifications and abide in the stillness of the Pure Awareness you really are, reaching the ultimate goal of your human experience.

The Swan Method will help you develop self-awareness and take spiritual responsibility for your reality, which in turn will organically shift, as you transform your perception and let go of the egoic need to control life that causes painful emotions. If you keep your mind directed inward, not only will you leave the past behind to be fully present, anchored in the flow of life; you will also give way to the light and love of the eternal Presence you are and have always been, finally recognizing that everything is perfect the way it is. Enjoy the journey!

THE PREMISE:
ONENESS

CHAPTER ONE

The Paradoxical Essence of Consciousness

God is everywhere and does everything. God is within us and knows everything. God is without us and sees everything. God is beyond us and is everything. God alone is.

— *Meher Baba*

One of my favorite Zen stories is that of Manjushri, the sage of supreme wisdom, arriving late to a gathering of fellow *bodhisattvas*, or awakened masters. When he got there, everyone had already left except for the Buddha and a young woman who was completely absorbed in a transcendental state. Surprised, Manjushri asked how it was possible that such a young student had attained such a profound state. "Bring her out of it," the Buddha suggested, "and ask her yourself."

The sage walked around her snapping his fingers, but she didn't budge. He gently tapped her shoulders, clapped his hands next to her ears, and even transported her to a higher realm to wake her up. It was all in vain; she remained undisturbed. Observing this, the Buddha realized the only one who could arouse her from this deep level of consciousness was Momyo, the *bodhisattva* of delusion. Once summoned, Momyo emerged from the depths of the earth. After bowing to his masters, he snapped his fingers at the woman and she immediately came out of meditation.

Momyo represents the knowledge of the external world that veils the reality of our divine nature. It is the ordinary consciousness that shapes our perception of life with memories, desires, and the attachment to people and things. You may think you are conscious because you can appreciate different situations, make choices, and interact with other beings, but you don't have any control over the way your life unfolds or the events that trigger negative impulses and emotions in you. For the most part, you simply *react* to life, driven by unconscious tendencies of perception that dictate your behavior.

Your attention is mainly on the outer world. You are busy with activities and obligations, tending to your personal needs and the needs of those you care for, spending most, if not all, of your time and energy seeking satisfaction and validation through your endeavors. These are natural aspects of your human adventure. Your search leads you to accumulate experiences and achieve your goals, but it also keeps you swinging between pleasure and pain as you run after desires that only yield more desires. This goes on for a long while, until you comprehend that the peace and happiness you yearn for can never be found outside of you.

Worldly pursuits rely on appearances and social recognition (success, wealth, power); they don't require self-awareness. But a more fulfilling self-expression demands honesty and integration to embrace who you are and what your life is about, to be at peace with yourself and others. Without inner peace, no matter how much success or wealth you may acquire, you remain dis-

The Paradoxical Essence of Consciousness

connected from life in some way, craving more of what you already have or what you think you need, in an attempt to fill an internal emptiness that seems endless.

Accomplishing your goals and fulfilling your desires are valuable pursuits that keep you going, but they don't help you understand what causes unpleasant events in your life, why you feel and react the way you do, or why you are compelled to chase one craving after another. They don't explain why a steady sense of contentment remains elusive and you only experience fleeting moments of enjoyment. They don't reveal what may prompt you to give your power away with self-destructive behaviors or negative habits that offer a temporary escape from a persistent, deep-seated restlessness.

Comprehending the paradoxical essence of Divine Consciousness, and how it infuses your experiences with meaning and purpose—through the challenges you encounter—turns your life into a journey of self-discovery toward emotional and spiritual freedom. But you have to step out of the usual perception of life as something external, material, and separate from you, by accepting it as a cosmic dream or play of Divine Consciousness that you don't need to fix or control. When you surrender to life as it is, you gradually uncover what lies beyond ordinary consciousness and get to experience the eternal joy of your divine nature.

The idea of anything being external, including God, arises from a deeply ingrained identification with the body and mind that creates the illusion of separation. This illusion colors our human perception at every level, thus distorting the true nature of reality. Some religions portray God as an authority figure deciding what is right or wrong through punishments and rewards, like a stern parent. These types of concepts have shaped rigid, dogmatic systems used to manipulate believers with the promise of redemption or salvation, yet they often benefit only those at the top of their hierarchical structures.

A less human-centric view of the infinite force inspiriting life can help you recognize that God does not need intermediaries, because God is the Divine Consciousness you are, along with everything else in the universe, and ultimately, that this universe is imaginary. This infinite Presence has been called *Purusha, Brahman, Paramatman, the Supreme Self, the Tao, Source, Krishna, Ishvara, Shiva, Rama, Allah, Yahweh, Hu, the Universal Mother, the Eternal Father, the King of Kings, God*, and a wealth of other names and titles that merely reflect different cultural expressions of the mysterious power that pervades all existence. Being infinite and all-encompassing, the Divine appears and can be conceived in myriad ways.

The spirits, entities, angels, archangels, avatars, deities, gods, goddesses, celestial beings, and ascended masters, as well as the enlightened saints of every spiritual tradition, represent the many forms and qualities of Divine Consciousness, which is pure light. Their rivals, so-called evil forces and demons, express the negative tendencies of the mind that veil or disturb the light, turning human life into a shadow play depicting an imaginary battle between light and darkness. Because our mind perceives and interprets everything according to its capacity, based on previous concepts and our identification with the physical body, we give human form to the energies or archetypes on both sides.

I use terms such as *Consciousness, Pure Awareness*, or the *Self* indistinctly to convey the pure, neutral quality of the Divine, as opposed to the transient aspects of the ego-mind. In this con-

The Paradoxical Essence of Consciousness

text, all the capitalized words throughout the book refer to this infinite principle, including the word *God* as the totality of existence rather than a separate Creator, since this timeless Presence pervades yet also transcends Creation.

The ancient Egyptians believed the world was originally water and darkness, like a womb, from which a blue lotus or a shiny egg sprang to reveal a sacred child whose light banished the darkness. He was the source of life—the Sun God or Creator. Similarly, in the Hindu traditions, the Divine Mother symbolizes the eternal Void or Cosmic Womb of pure potentiality from which everything emerges, including the deities Brahma, Vishnu, and Shiva, who represent the creative, sustaining, and destructive or transforming principles of Consciousness inherent in all life. In both cultures, as in many others, life itself was born out of the absolute, unmanifest reality.

The Unmanifest precedes all manifestations. And yet, in the world of duality and polarities, God has been reduced to externalized forms, leading humans to argue and wage wars over the different concepts and attributes to which they have become attached, unaware that the highest spiritual goal is to realize the Divine as the unifying force of the universe—the eternal Self we all are and everything is. We achieve this goal individually, through self-knowledge, devotion, or spiritual disciplines leading to superconscious or blissful states, where Pure Awareness clears the delusion of separation.

Removing the division seems to be the primary purpose of non-dualistic or pantheistic sources of wisdom, but even in the dualistic devotional paths, the idea of being separate from God creates great distress, expressing a deep yearning for a sacred or mystical union, which is the true meaning of *yoga*. In reality, this union is not between two separate entities; it is reclaiming our very essence. Duality strives for unity or Oneness. The human soul longs to merge with the Supreme Soul. That which is manifest wants to return to its original state of undivided, timeless, pure *being*.

Religions teach people how to follow moral standards to live in the human dreamworld, offering definitions of God or the promise of better dreamworlds in other planes of experience, but they cannot grant the realization of your divine nature, where all divisions and suffering disappear. Only you can achieve it in yourself, by yourself, as you awaken from your dream, on your own. This process requires breaking free from the constrictions of the mind and the ideas of God as an external parental figure, which will become clearer later on, once you understand how what I call your *sense of otherness* maintains this delusion of duality and separation.

Divine Consciousness cannot be constrained to any particular form, and yet, it appears as every possible form. It also gives you the capacity to comprehend the external world and relate to the Supreme in your individual way. The same force that creates and sustains the universe motivates the inquisitive mind of a scientist to explain the cosmos. It inspires the creative drive of a musician or an artist or a writer to give expression to the human condition. It fuels the passion of a visionary to promote wellness and balance or equality and justice. It also manifests through everything you feel, hear, see, touch, taste, think, and experience, as well as the choices you make and everything you do, imagine, and learn.

You cannot prove or measure the existence of Divine Consciousness; it is a mystery far beyond the limitations of the mental and material realms. Those who believe in God cannot prove God's existence, and those who don't believe are also unable to prove that God doesn't exist. Wanting proof is like asking a fish to demonstrate the reality of water, even though the fish couldn't live without it. Consciousness is not perceivable because it is what makes perception possible. Your spiritual awakening is an intimate experience beyond sensory perception.

You don't have to prove your own existence; you simply know that *you are*. This *I-am-ness* transcends the mind; it is an absolute truth that does not rely on anything, not even time or space, since these are mental concepts. The certainty of *being* is internal, subjective. It arises in the Pure Awareness you are that precedes thoughts while making everything appear real. But to comprehend this truth, you have to seek what lies beyond ordinary consciousness, opening up to a non-cognitive, heart-centered perception that dissolves the ignorance preventing you from realizing what you truly are. When you cultivate self-awareness, you redirect the mind inward, gradually removing all divisions until you are able to see the Divine everywhere: in those you have loved and those you have hated; in the so-called good and the so-called evil; in all creation and destruction; in light and darkness; in nature and all living creatures; and in the breath and flow of life itself.

Divine Consciousness is the absolute harmony of Feminine and Masculine, *yin* and *yang*, stillness and movement. The desire to experience itself is the original thought that splits these aspects and configures the dream of Creation as a multiplicity of forms, thus giving rise to duality. The Divine Masculine is the Consciousness principle directing life with its magnetic force, and the Divine Feminine is the principle of Primordial Matter or creative potentiality that crystallizes Consciousness in all shapes and attributes. This is how the Supreme Self experiences itself in all possible forms, in a continuous, eternal unfolding.

Although essentially one and the same, Consciousness and Matter become the interdependent aspects of the cosmic dream. The first manifestation of their interplay is the Cosmic Mind expressing itself as "I am," which becomes the ego in the human mind. This original I-thought creates all other thoughts, shaping your private dreamworld by hijacking the role of the eternal Self as the true director. Objects appear separate because of the individualizing principle we call *ego*, when in reality they are appearances of the eternal Self, which embraces all there is, all there has ever been, and all there will ever be.

The Self shapes and moves the universe, like an invisible magnet, by imagining or dreaming itself in infinite possibilities of expression while keeping perfectly still and undisturbed. When you are dreaming or daydreaming, you can imagine a variety of scenarios and interactions that arise from within you—from memories, thoughts, and desires. You may lose yourself in that state, but only momentarily. It takes much longer to awaken from the divine dreamworld you consider your reality, because you identify with sensory perception; however, it all emerges from within you, as thoughts. The paradox here is that the eternal Self casts the illusion of a false I-sense or ego appearing as the material world, where all sorts of dramas take place, while the Self remains unaffected, simply dreaming a cosmic dream.

Your soul is a spark of Consciousness, an individualized expression in the dreamworld; your mind is the screen where Consciousness is projected and filtered, and your physical body is a byproduct of the ego that grants you the experience of the

The Paradoxical Essence of Consciousness

dreamworld. Your subjective-objective perception of life results from the interplay of the elements and qualities of nature (known as *gunas*) through which the Divine Feminine keeps the cosmic dream going. In this sense, the creative Matter principle is both the vehicle of the Consciousness principle and also what veils it with individualized experiences. The world is considered an illusion (*Maya*) because nothing in it is permanent or conscious; it evolves from the ignorance that produces a multiplicity of forms concealing the totality of the Self.

The Divine is the only timeless and unchanging reality there is. Every tangible and intangible phenomenon in the universe is a projection of Consciousness materializing through its creative potential. A good analogy is the light radiating from the sun. You could say it is the sun, and you could also say it is not the sun, since the light is a projection of the sun and does not exist without the sun. Then again, the sun is a transformation of cosmic matter, just like a tree is the modification of a seed or a mountain a variation of the earth. Every object evolves from something else and cannot exist on its own or by itself. Only the Supreme Self is a perennial, absolute reality.

The world is illusory because everything in it is relative and continually changing into something else. All objects are modifications of other objects and are bound to experience further transformations as well. They are impermanent; they appear, change, and disappear. How can something be real when it comes and goes? Your personal dreamworld is also a temporary illusion because it is a creation of your mind within the cosmic dream of Consciousness. Every single aspect evolves according to its function, in perfect synchronicity with everything else. You may think you are effecting these changes, but they happen without your control, as the dream of Consciousness unfolds into eternity.

Your mind translates these changes as sensory impressions through your ego, which is the false I-sense that thinks, "I am the one seeing, feeling, touching, or *doing* this, so this is *my* experience." However, it is all a projection of Consciousness that the mind conceptualizes, labels, and identifies with to create the sense of experience. The world is not separate from you, because it does not exist apart from your mental perception making it real. What you believe to be tangible and solid disappears when you are asleep, if you go into a superconscious state or a coma, or when your body dies. These external aspects are as temporary as your dreams; they only arise with your consciousness.

Your knowledge of the world is the accumulation of thoughts and impressions from previous experiences. You may think that something does not exist simply because it hasn't left an imprint on your mind. Once it does, by contact with the physical senses, by imagination, inference, or awareness, its memory remains and is now added to the psychic reservoir that shapes your overall view of reality. You associate certain memories and thoughts with similar impressions, both consciously and unconsciously, and make assumptions based on them as well.

Your overall perception of life follows the same principle. As experiences leave mental imprints, and these repeat within a variety of contexts, they create dynamic tendencies of thought and action that color future events. So, although life is continuous change and fluctuation, how you interpret and experience it depends on your past impressions and memories. These hinder your ability to live fully in the present, limiting your capacity to enjoy life as it happens, without expecting it to be any different. At the same time, because of your divine essence, these restrictions prompt you to seek a way out of your self-created limitations.

The paradox here is that the Supreme Self projects the world to experience itself through your mind while gradually driving you to dissolve the mental mirage of the world that blocks its absolute Reality. So, just like your dreams feel real in the dream state, with people, places, and situations appearing three-dimensional and real, your life is a personal dream or movie where people, objects, and events become individualized sensory experiences. It is like going on a roller-coaster ride that takes you through a variety of situations and emotions, only to realize at the end of the ride that you haven't moved at all, because it was all your imagination.

Another way of looking at it is as a game of hide-and-seek, where Divine Consciousness is concealed behind its material reflections while also looking for itself as their source. Your life is a smaller scale version of this game. Your physical reality is made of contrasting layers of light and energy that appear three-dimensional to you, just like a movie, a painting, or a photograph seem real on a flat surface. Your senses translate these layers of light into tangible objects and sensations, as well as distinct scenarios and events organized in space and time.

It is by the agency of the ego that the mind objectifies your true Self as the world, making it feel separate from you. But there is no separation; you are the subject appearing as a variety of phenomena, such as your body, your mind, people, places, objects, and so on. Everything you go through to grow and individuate gradually leads you back to your essential Oneness, where the illusion of an individual identity dissolves. Then, and only then, can you perceive the world as the totality you are, rather than as something external and divided.

This, of course, entails a process of increasing self-awareness, introspection, and reflection. You are a spark of the Divine on a scavenger hunt for experiences. You evolve as you explore the possibilities of your human existence, along with the suffering that comes with it, until you comprehend that the happiness you seek demands a process of *involution*, or inwardness, to reclaim your divine nature.

It may seem absurd to think of human beings as Divine Consciousness when we witness so much hatred and injustice in the world. Indeed, rather than trying to find our essence, we have been dwelling in pain and ignorance, performing all kinds of selfish acts. Some people get angry at God for allowing so much misery in the world, or deny God's existence because of it. Even those on a spiritual path often wonder, why did the Divine choose to undergo human desires, emotions, and pain, if it is self-sustained, self-fulfilling, eternal peace?

The desire of the Supreme Self to imagine itself in endless shapes and forms is a mystery that cannot be appreciated with the mind. As great sages have stated, *to understand God, you must become God*. What gets in the way of your true nature is the identification with the body and mind; this false identity is your ego. From this ego consciousness, it is impossible to comprehend that the Divine does not suffer, that suffering happens in the mind only, and that its very purpose is to redirect the mind inward toward the Inner Self, where there is no pain.

As you remove the false ideas of individuality and division, you perceive the perfection of life, where everything is what it needs to be for the purpose of guiding you toward your totality as Pure Awareness. You may observe a single cell with a microscope or widen your view to see it as part of a complex, dynamic organism. Likewise, you can fixate on an experience as something isolated or you can expand your perception to understand the overall meaning of the events in your life. Each experience has led you to another experience, which has also led you to another one, and another one, to bring you to where you are now.

Just like every cell is self-directed to fulfill its function within the organism as a whole, every appearance of Consciousness is also self-directed to fulfill its purpose within the totality you are. In other words, things are exactly as they are meant to be; Consciousness simply takes innumerable appearances without ever being affected or tainted by any of them. We humanize our ideas of God, but God is not human. God does not micromanage the world, which is a projection of the ego; we are responsible for the inequality and pain we create with our individual and collective choices. But that self-created suffering exists only at the level of the ego consciousness. It is a trick of the ego to judge or blame the Divine, for this reinforces the delusion of duality that gives the ego its virtual existence.

The eternal Self is infinite peace, joy and bliss; it does not lack or need anything. You crave love, happiness, and freedom because these are aspects of your original nature, but the constant stream of thoughts and desires flooding your mind prompt you to look for them outside of yourself. The nature of desire is dissatisfaction; it arises from the feeling of deficiency that is inherent in the ego as the individualizing principle that disconnects you from Divine Consciousness. The contentment you feel when a desire is fulfilled doesn't come from the outcome of it but from a momentary *absence* of desire. That brief pause from a sense of lack gives you a taste of your true nature, although the ego swiftly creates new desires to disrupt it again and again.

Anything other than Consciousness is a transitory projection, a mirage bound to cause pain—until you see it for what it is. Desires fuel the choices that cause, heal, or avert suffering now and in the future. Through suffering, you learn to accept and forgive yourself and others. It shows you your limitations, prodding you to mature emotionally and spiritually as you overcome every obstacle, challenge, and loss. This is how we learn and grow in the world of polarities, where one experience often leads to its opposite: birth gives way to death, and death brings rebirth; pleasure results in pain, and pain yields dispassion, which eventually liberates us from all the polarities.

These manifestations are part of a self-directed play where everything happens on its own yet is also the result of something else. A fruit bears its own seeds of re-creation; each seed holds the creative potential to produce new seeds and fruits and trees. You can think of each fruit as something new or as a modification of the previous objects out of which that fruit came to be: a seed, a flower, or a tree, as well as the other elements and factors that contributed to its existence. These also resulted from the transformation of something that followed a similar process. Nothing can exist in isolation; the whole universe takes part in every single event.

An apple may come and go; it may appear and then disappear; it may go through many changes as it develops, ripens, and then dissolves; it is essentially impermanent. However, the life force that produced it is perennial and continues producing new forms. This is the only *constant* among all the manifestations of nature. Consciousness pervades all life while remaining hidden, like the sun behind its sunbeams. The air you breathe, the water you drink, the food you eat; the things you smell, taste, touch, feel, and hear; the thoughts, desires, and feelings with which you identify; and everything you perceive and experience—these are all modifications of Consciousness dreaming the world in your mind through the elements and qualities of its creative principle. These are the *gunas* known as *sattva*, *rajas*, and *tamas*. They shape the universe like strands weaving the fabric of life.

Sattva is light, purity, and peace. It is the aspect of Pure Awareness through which you perceive everything, and it is also the main quality you need to cultivate to awaken from the dream. *Rajas* is activity, change, impulse, and movement. It is the driving force that manifests in the mind as desire, attraction, passion, longing, and attachment, through which the objective reality remains active. *Tamas* is the energy of inertia, darkness, or inactivity emerging from the spiritual ignorance of the absolute reality of the Self. It gives the world its material density and stability, but in excess it can lead to stagnation, dullness, and depression. When the light of Consciousness (*sattva*) counters this dark quality, objects appear tangible and three-dimensional. Ultimately, you could say that *sattva* creates the world, *tamas* obscures it, and *rajas* distorts it.

These natural energies are in continuous interaction with each other in all aspects of life, including your psycho-physiological changes and mental processes, as well as the types of foods, activities, and environments you choose. In balance, they support one another. If out of balance, *tamas* becomes dullness or stagnation and *rajas* turns into restlessness, anxiety, or aggression. For instance, to go into meditation, *sattva* must be predominant, which requires the restless mind to quiet down and the physical body to keep steady without falling asleep. That is, the qualities of activity and inactivity have to counter each other to create stability for *sattva* to increase as you concentrate on the object of meditation until your mind merges with it.

If you comprehend that your reality is the dynamic interplay of these energies producing fluctuations and change, then you can accept that everything is Divine Consciousness unfolding by its own accord. You can disbelieve the egoic illusion of "doership" and "ownership" that taints your perception with attachments and fears. Furthermore, to reclaim your original nature (*sattva*), you have to break free from your ignorance (*tamas*) and self-importance (*rajas*) by dissolving your identification with the body and mind. Both mind and body are vehicles for the world of forms, but you are neither your body nor your mind; you are the one who observes them.

There is no greater teacher than life. When you see the purpose behind all its ups and downs, your perception spontaneously shifts to embrace it fully and openly. The paradox here is that you are essentially perfect and yet a continuous work in progress. You are absolutely free yet also trapped in a mind-body complex, longing for freedom from the limitations through which you perceive yourself. And you are undergoing a slow, restricted, egocentric expedition to discover your potential as you evolve and involve. In other words, *you are a unique experience of the Self in search of yourself.*

You approach life from an individualized vantage point that reflects your journey, and nobody else can perceive it exactly the same way. But you are made of the same divine substance as every other being, struggling with the same ego as the rest of humanity, and yearning to transcend the same suffering. You do it by following a path set with events over which you have no real control, and you experience them according to your own memories and impressions. And yet, your ultimate goal is to clear the illusion of separation to realize that you and others are one with All-There-Is.

A skilled sculptor can see the figure waiting to emerge from a stone before working on it. Chiseling out what does not belong, the artist brings forth their vision into reality. Your path is no different, except that you are the stone, the sculpture, and the sculptor transforming one into the other. But you start in the dark and gain greater clarity as you excise everything you are not, because it causes you pain. Again, the real artist is the eternal Self directing your process from within, but it appears as if your mind and body are doing all the work.

Spirituality is self-knowledge, which requires self-awareness and humility to remove the ego that blocks your light. As you embark on an inward journey of self-discovery, you uncover the wounded aspects you have been hiding from yourself. As a unique expression of the Divine, you are the traveler, the journey, and the destination. Only you can walk the path paved with the choices you have made and continue to make as it unfolds. Only you can transform your experience of reality by taking responsibility for your perception. Only you can investigate your mind to remove everything you are *not* but believe that you are—your false ideas, outdated beliefs, and negative emotions and habits.

There are no shortcuts in this process, but as you surrender to the fluid, paradoxical nature of Consciousness, you navigate life more gracefully. In spite of the sense of separation and isolation produced by your ego, you are never alone. How can you be alone when you are All-There-Is? Beyond the entrapment of sensory perception, you are always guided and supported on your journey, in accordance with Divine Law, or *Dharma*. The events you experience gradually help you discern between your true Self and your non-Self—or ego—as you cultivate dispassion for the world of appearances to find the truth within.

During the many cycles of development and integration you undergo, swinging between pleasure and pain, you create and resolve painful dynamics with others until you achieve the spiritual maturity to comprehend that there is no separation, and that nothing is real but the Self. You cannot reclaim your divinity without clearly seeing what has been obstructing it, so it is helpful to understand the various aspects creating your experiences in the dreamworld, as well as the distortions causing you pain.

* * *

Developing Stillness

This is a short exercise to start developing mental silence or stillness. Obviously, just reading about it will not do much; you have to develop the discipline to take breaks through the day to practice it for five to ten minutes, being as consistent as possible.

Find a quiet place to sit where you will not get interrupted. Close your eyes and be aware of any external sounds, body sensations, emotions, and thoughts. Take a deep breath to relax and leave all these distractions out there. Then bring your attention to your heart and direct your breathing here, keeping your inhalations slow and smooth, and your exhalations steady and long. This is all you have to do for now: anchoring your breathing in your heart for five to ten minutes as much as possible during the course of your day.

The Paradoxical Essence of Consciousness

As simple as this may sound, your mind will distract you time and again. You will forget to do it or thoughts will get in the way while you are doing it, making you feel that you should be doing more or doing something else or that something is missing. Your main effort here is refusing to follow any mental activity for those five to ten minutes, which you are certainly not used to doing. If thoughts or sensations come up, do not judge, follow, or try to control them; just take a deep breath to regain your center by bringing your attention and breathing back to your heart. In time, your steady concentration will exclude everything else.

No matter how pleasant, persistent, or distressful, thoughts and sensations are just mental fluctuations of energy. If you don't pay attention, they will fade away. But if you let them pull you outward, you reinforce them, not only during this practice, but also in your daily life. Keep redirecting your mind inward through this exercise; everything else will still be there when you are done. If you take a pause from your activities to do this regularly, you will become more balanced and self-aware while interacting with the world.

This practice leaves *sattvic* imprints of neutrality and peace that will allow you to go deeper during meditation as well. It is also very helpful during stressful times. If you start making excuses to skip these centering breaks or get pulled away with other things, simply go back to this discipline as soon as you realize you are putting it off.

CHAPTER TWO

The Complex Nature of Your Soul

> *We are like silkworms; we make the thread out of our own substance and spin the cocoon, and in course of time are imprisoned within it. But this is not forever. In that cocoon we shall develop spiritual realization and, like the butterfly, come out free.*
> — *Swami Vivekananda*

In Plato's famous "Allegory of the Cave," Socrates asks Plato's brother to imagine a group of people forced to spend their lives chained inside a cave, unable to move or look at anything other than a wall in front of them. An enormous fire burns behind them, on a higher level, and there is a walkway between the fire and the prisoners watching the wall. Other people walk and talk along this corridor, carrying things on their heads, such as artifacts and statues made of different materials.

As the prisoners see the shadows of those objects projected onto the wall and hear the echoes of the voices behind them, they take these projections for their reality. How they relate to each other and what they talk about is based on this collective delusion. According to Socrates, if a man were to free himself from the chains, turn around, and look at the fire, he would be blinded by the light, unable to see what he had previously known to be real. If he chose to leave the cave, he would have to become accustomed to the light and the sight of the upper world that had been non-existent until that point.

Then he would discern the shadows, the reflections of people and objects, as well as the people and objects themselves. He could gaze at the sun, the moon, and the stars in the sky, realizing that his former view of reality was distorted. However, if he returned to the cave to share his new appreciation of the truth, those still enslaved to the wall would likely be too afraid to question the only life they have known, seeing him either as a fool or a threat.

Plato uses this allegory to highlight the sharp contrast between philosophical knowledge and the ignorance of the general population. But it can be applied to the quest for spiritual truth as well. Like the prisoners in the cave, your human experience is limited by the sensory perception you identify with, which is tainted with past impressions projected as your reality. You can only free yourself from this phenomenological, shadow-like existence with the light of Pure Awareness, clearing outdated ideas and beliefs to access a higher perception.

It starts by appreciating that you are not fixed. You are not *this* or *that*. You are an appearance of Consciousness in continuous expansion, yet trapped in the identification with your body and mind. You escape your own "mental cave" by shedding light onto the distortions of your false identity, peeling away layer after layer of ignorance to make more room for the truth. To realize the Self, you have to understand what is not the Self, so you can stop objectifying yourself and seeing the world as something external.

The Complex Nature of Your Soul

The ancient sages of India perceived various dimensions of the soul, from highest to lowest. The Supreme Soul (*Paramatma*) is the Soul of Souls, the universal aspect with absolute knowledge and no attributes; it is the Supreme Self or unmanifest, Pure Consciousness or Awareness. The Inner Self or Spirit (*Antaratma*) is a modification of the Supreme Soul within Creation or the dreamworld; it is identical in nature, but it is projected as the individual soul (*Atma*), enveloped in energy layers to transmigrate from one physical body to another. In reality, there is no separation, and the different dimensions of the soul can be conceived as gradations of Consciousness, in the sense of varying degrees of purity, light, or planes of awareness.

Think of the Supreme Soul as the ocean, the Inner Self as the seawater, and the individual soul as seawater trapped in a temporary glass bottle floating in the ocean and bumping into other bottles. We are all the One Supreme Self, and yet every soul is a unique yet complex compound of energy layers shaped by a distinct journey. Each soul is a singular expression of Consciousness encapsulated in various sheaths that hold and express memories, impressions, and desires left by previous experiences. These filter the light of Awareness to become the mental functions creating the material reality where you act, feel, judge, reflect, learn, grow, and produce things that appear separate and organized in space and time.

These energy layers are like nesting shades filtering the light of the Self projected as your consciousness of physical, mental, and emotional objects and events. They are known as the *causal body*, the *subtle body*, and the *gross body*. The subtle and causal bodies form the psyche, which is the totality of the mind—our human cognitive consciousness. The Sanskrit term for it is *antahkarana*, which means the "internal" (*antah*) instruments or functions that create the illusion of individualized, external phenomena through which the Self experiences itself. For this reason, it is often symbolized as a revolving wheel with four spokes that represent the objective mind, the intellect, the ego, and the field of experience.

The Inner Self is the hub or center of the wheel animating all movement through your internal and external instruments of perception and action while remaining perfectly still. In this context, the gross body is a creation or projection of the mind that serves as its vehicle of expression; it dies at the end of its karmic timeline. The subtle body is a projection of the causal body; it merges back with it at the end of each lifetime until it eventually dissolves, after many incarnations, in the pure knowledge of the Self. The causal body transmigrates from birth to birth as the subtle content and container of the mind; it merges with its cosmic source when the liberated soul drops the last physical body, completely free from all identifications, desires, and karma.

Although each aspect can be viewed as the modification of other aspects, they work together as a whole to shape your human experience. However, exploring them separately can help you understand the nature of your reality and shift your perception toward greater harmony between all the elements of your psyche. This requires self-awareness, honesty, and mindfulness, because ordinary consciousness fluctuates as you react to things, but it also tends to get stuck in outdated patterns of thought. Let's take a closer look at each of these energy sheaths, from the densest to the subtlest.

THE GROSS BODY

The physical body is a temporary projection that serves as the vehicle of expression for the mind, providing opportunities to experience the material plane and contribute to it in some way. The external senses are receptive windows of perception that, along with the organs of action (larynx, hands, feet, genitals, and anus), as well as the psycho-physiological functions of the body, give you the illusion of being a separate person; this is your ego attaching the mind to sensory perception. All of these aspects are modifications of the *gunas* through which the creative principle of Consciousness shapes your reality. Although you are an appearance of the eternal Self, when the body dies, the idea of being the individual you believe yourself to be also dies.

The body is made of the elements of the earth and sustained by its nutrients; it is the "food body" and cannot survive or thrive without proper nourishment. There is no ordinary consciousness without a body, so taking good care of it is important, making sure it is balanced and vibrant, which also requires taking good care of the planet. The body relies on *prana*—the vital force that inspirits your human journey. If you want to be healthy and clear, it is best to avoid substances that pollute or block your life force, such as drugs and alcohol, as well as air, water, and food deprived of energy due to impurities, poor nutrients, chemicals, microwaves, genetic modifications, or radiation. A balanced vegetarian or vegan diet, as well as respecting all sentient beings while avoiding forceful or violent actions promotes the *sattvic* quality that purifies body and mind for spiritual growth.

Because the physical body is the vehicle of expression of the mind, and the mind identifies with the body, you believe that you are your body and mind; this is a false identity. I will explore in more detail why it cannot be the real you, but for now think of the body as an aspect of your external reality. It has no volition of its own; it is ruled by the psyche that regulates your physiological functions and mental processes with instinctual, unconscious, and conscious impulses. Scientists study the brain to understand the mind-body connection, because the brain decodes and connects the mind to the physical body. But without a causal and a subtle body to direct it, a brain is just a lump of matter with no impact, just like a physical body without prana is a compound of lifeless tissues.

However, there is a continuous interplay between your physical and mental aspects. Healthy foods and habits of thought and action purify body and mind, thus establishing a harmonious, unified sense of self for the full expression of your soul. Your body translates the energy of your inner and outer worlds into physical sensations and impressions, triggering thoughts, feelings, desires, and expectations that color your perception of reality. It may also express symptoms or illnesses to reflect mental-emotional issues you may be hiding or suppressing. Disease does not result only from suppression, since it can be caused by other factors, but unresolved emotions play a significant role in the susceptibility to those factors and the causation of pathology. Be conscientious of how you treat your body and listen to it to promote balance. You need a strong body supporting a strong mind to pursue your goals.

Now, caring for it is important, but getting too attached to your body traps you in low levels of awareness. It is your vehicle of expression in the world, but it is also the furthest layer from the Inner Self. Keep it active and healthy to enjoy the mobility and experiences it provides, while remembering that it is made of the earth and follows the laws of the earth. It develops, transforms, declines, and dies, like everything else on this plane. Accept the aging process and view your illnesses as the price of embodying a physical form, like the rent you pay to live in a house or the maintenance for your car.

When the awareness gets stuck at the level of the gross body, sensory perception is strongest. You believe yourself to be your body and fully identify with your sensations and impressions. This is vital when you are a young child, to voice your needs or discomfort, and in general to avoid harmful things; beyond that, you may become overly attached to food, comfort, and sensual pleasure or obsessed with your physical appearance. The fear of death, which is the natural attachment to life from your identification with the body, is the root of all other fears. Remember that it is a vehicle, ready to take you places, yet in need of a driver to give it direction. Since it cannot operate without the subtle body, when you identify with it, it means your level of awareness is mainly in the lower mind or ego consciousness.

THE SUBTLE BODY

The subtle or astral body consists of the various aspects of the mind and the energy layer attaching the mind to the physical body. Although they don't operate independently, understanding their separate functions is useful to recognize how your ego consciousness fluctuates to hide the truth of who you are, and why you react the way you do. Since I explore the ego in more detail throughout the book, I am including just a brief overview of it here.

The Energy Layer

This is the sheath of prana, the energy that holds the soul together and binds the subtle layers to the physical body at each incarnation. It activates the functioning of your external senses and psycho-physiological processes, regulating your organism as a whole, and providing movement for mental and physical expression. Prana is the blood of the universe; it sustains the physical body through the air, water, and food you take in to nourish your blood, which in turn feeds all other tissues and systems. It is the force that keeps you alive, as it flows through your body, subtle channels, and energy centers, linking your existence to the earth, the cosmos, and all internal and external manifestations of Consciousness.

Since prana is in charge of the overall functioning of your body and mind, healing is really about removing what may be disrupting its flow. Holistic, energy-based systems and practices aim to increase it to promote mental clarity and physical health. Homeopathy, Chinese medicine, and Ayurveda, as well as healing methods and practices focused on increasing energy, are more effective at restoring wellness than attempting to suppress isolated symptoms, which is what conventional medicine tends to do. This type of system is useful in an emergency, the need for surgery, or a life-or-death situation, but if a sick person isn't treated as a whole, to promote homeostasis, their cellular intelligence will keep producing physical symptoms to signal that something is out of balance.

Toxic substances harm the energy body because they circulate in the blood stream, polluting the flow of prana, thus affecting the mind and other tissues, organs, and systems. More energy means more vitality, longevity, and clarity. This sheath links the physical body to the subtle body through the breath, which is essential for human life. If you control the breath, you control the mind. When your mind is restless or anxious, your breathing is restricted and shallow. When your mind is calmer, your breathing becomes lighter and expansive, which further relaxes your body.

Healing requires relaxation, because tension and stress disrupt the flow of prana. In deep meditation, your breathing can become so subtle that it seems to stop; there is less air and more prana promoting overall rejuvenation. It also slows down during sleep, which is a resting period for cleansing and recharging. There are many breathing techniques to generate energy, quiet the mind, and access deeper meditative states, but even just being aware of your breathing on a regular basis, making it deep, slow, and rhythmic, promotes greater vitality and peace.

This layer is immaterial and neutral, but it is also the driving force behind all aspects of life and all activity in the body. It is both invisible and visible, since it results in movement, action, and change. It becomes more apparent when you come out of meditation or a complete immersion in a creative endeavor and feel an energetic "high" that raises your mental state and makes you feel more alive. Also, when you get excited about something, or after breathing practices or breath-related activities like singing or exercising, since there is more prana flowing through you. Another clear expression of it happens right after childbirth, when the space is filled with the vital force of a brand new human being.

By contrast, if your energy is stagnant or scattered, it shows in negative ways, such as dullness, stiffness, depression, anxiety, confusion, restlessness, and all sorts of ailments. You counter this with disciplines that increase prana, such as *pranayama*, yoga postures focused on the breath, *tai chi*, *qigong*, and similar methods, including martial arts centered on mindfulness, since they promote the alignment of the mind with the breath. When the body reaches its karmic span at the end of each incarnation, the soul retrieves all its prana to disconnect the psychic sheaths from the physical plane and continue its journey.

The Mental Layers

The mind is the field of experience where your life unfolds. Like a mirror, it takes the shape of different objects and situations through the qualities of nature. It is not the mind but the light of Consciousness projected on the mind that gives you cognitive faculties. The mind is not conscious in itself; it is the screen that reflects the world. The sense of experience results from the interaction of the lower mind, the higher mind, and the ego actualizing predominant seeds of perception from your causal body.

The Objective or Lower Mind

The lower mind is the receptive, recording faculty that receives impressions through the physical senses and rules motor and sensory organs. It is the more objective or "outer" aspect of the mind that gathers information, recognizing and interacting with the world of forms. It is the day-to-day, ordinary consciousness that can function almost automatically, through the power of habit, when you are not mindful or fully present in what you are doing.

The soul layers are gradations of Consciousness that hold high and low levels of light, depending on which elements each interacts or overlaps with. The aspect of the lower mind closest to the gross body is activated by instinctual impulse and sensory perception, while the highest level relates to emotional intelligence. This is the function through which you let the world in and *feel* things, but it requires the higher mind or intellect to process, judge, and discern these impressions in order to take action or come to a decision. For instance, you may confuse love with lust, attachment, affection, or sensual pleasure unless you are able to differentiate them.

The objective mind receives the input from the external world, but it can create contradictions and confusion between desire, illusion, and reality. It is more psycho-emotional than rational, taking the world in through the physical senses; it can also perceive the energy behind words, attitudes, motivations, subliminal messages, and hidden emotions or motivations, although none of these are evaluated at this level. Clarity and understanding require the piercing quality of the intellect to judge things accurately, process ideas and emotions, and discriminate between intuition and fantasy, truth and deceit.

This aspect perceives the world through the sensitivity of the physical body and the impressions of previous experiences. It is considered the "conscious mind" because it carries your thoughts, words, and actions during the wakeful state, as opposed to the sleep or dream states. However, it is mainly receptive and unconscious, and it does not differentiate between what is real or imagined, true or false. At this level, you absorb information and discern objects, words, ideas, and feelings without evaluating their meaning or veracity, or making associations between them.

Without the discrimination of the intellect, the lower mind is like a receptacle that takes whatever comes in as the truth, just like you did when you were a young child. You've had to develop the higher mind to process information, learn things, make choices, and know yourself. You can think of the lower, objective mind as the mental-emotional cognitive capacity that is devoid of reflection, mindfulness, or wisdom. For this reason, it is the aspect over which the ego has the most control. At this level of awareness, you identify with your impulses and emotions, seeking pleasure and trying to avoid painful sensations and feelings with rationalizations, distractions, or addictions.

If the awareness fixates here because the higher mind is underdeveloped or clouded by alcohol, drugs, fear, pain, passion, or negative emotions, there is a complete identification with the impulsive dictates of the physical senses without restraint or self-awareness. This is why people do things they may later regret, ranging from yelling, arguing, lying, or cheating to stealing, hurting, and killing. The behavior becomes destructive when the ability to discern right from wrong and truth from illusion gets blurry, either during drug-induced states or due to an excessive flow of thoughts and desires overpowering the higher mind.

The Ego

Within the mental field, the ego creates the illusion of doership and ownership that turns every situation into *your* experience. It is the principle of individuality giving you a sense of identity through your identification with the physical body; it also produces the illusion of separation from what appears external and, most importantly, from your divine nature. In yogic or spiritual terms, the ego hijacks the Self as the *experiencer* of life, even though it is a projection of the Self as different forms and qualities.

The ego dominates the lower, psycho-emotional layer of the mind directly linked to the physical senses, which is prone to following instinctual or base impulses. Until you develop self-awareness, by redirecting the mind inward, the ego controls your perception and behavior, creating a gap between your intellectual understanding and your unconscious, emotional reactions. Since it is shaped in the early years, before the higher mind is developed, the ego taints your self-perception with the fears and emotional codependency of childhood.

I use the term *ego-mind* to refer to this compound of lower mind and ego where the ego rules your behavior with impulsive desires, attachments, and fears, in contrast with the discriminative capacity of the higher mind. Although the intellect is also directed by the ego, it is the function you use to process thoughts and experiences, understand the truth, and redirect your attention inward, which eventually dissolves the ego in its source.

The Intellect or Higher Mind

The Higher Mind is the sheath of wisdom. It is the judging faculty that gives you the ability to process the impressions of the lower mind and the physical senses, as well as the capacity to remember and learn from your experiences and intellectual pursuits. This is where Divine Consciousness is projected to direct your perception and actions, which makes you believe your mind is conscious when in reality it is just the screen where the Self manifests as the world of forms. Since it is the closest to the spiritual layer in the causal body, this mental sheath also has a receptive, intuitive quality that transcends cognitive functions. For this reason, the higher mind can help clear the path to spiritual freedom, even though Self-realization is not achieved through intellectual prowess but the earnest yearning for the Divine.

In Sanskrit, this aspect is called *buddhi*, which comes from *budh*, a term encompassing the ideas of awakening or being awake; of observing, learning, knowing, or becoming aware or conscious. The word *Buddha* is derived from it to convey prince Siddhartha's full spiritual awakening. The intellect processes the information from the psycho-emotional mind to judge, learn, and make choices; it also reflects the heart's intelligence that expresses the wisdom of your true nature. As the greatest spiritual masters have stated, *when the mind is directed outward, it creates the world; when it is directed inward, it leads to the Self.*

By the agency of the ego, the higher mind identifies with the physical senses and becomes aware of itself. Unlike the lower mind, it has a discriminative quality that grants you the capacity to discern between what is true or false; what is past or present; what is real or imaginary; and what brings you suffering or peace. This also gives you the willpower to detach and redirect your attention to accomplish both worldly and spiritual goals and to explore and master the ego-mind.

However, when the ego makes a home here, so to speak, you may be trapped in your mind, trusting only your intellectual capacity, which disjoints your experience of life as a whole and often alienates those around you. For instance, you may use your knowledge to psychoanalyze, judge, or manipulate others instead of empathizing with them on an emotional level; you may feel superior because of your intelligence or achievements while disconnecting from your humanity. This is why someone can be a genius in the realm of abstract ideas yet completely lost when it comes to social interactions. If the capacity to feel is blocked, they may *think* they are happy without actually experiencing joy, living instead in a state of rational apathy and lack of self-awareness. It is like having a chemical understanding of sugar without ever tasting its sweetness.

The ego dwells in this layer with a sense of self-importance or intellectual arrogance as a protective mechanism to hide unresolved emotions or destructive tendencies. A person may dismiss anything that is not material, measurable, or logical. Or they may use their knowledge and intuition to acquire power over others, if given the opportunity. At the extreme, human life is perceived as a series of physiochemical reactions in the brain and human desires and actions as phenomena to be studied, classified, or controlled.

At the same time, the desire to learn and contribute something, by pursuing your goals, also arises here, fueled by the drive to share the unique expression of your soul. Depending on your level of spiritual maturity, it may follow higher principles or get tainted with the egoic need for validation. The higher mind provides the discipline and focus to accomplish things, as well as the ability to process information, as you learn about yourself and the world. In addition, through the experience of transcendental states, its discriminating quality gradually dissolves the illusion of separation created by the ego, which increases the longing for inner peace. A deeper transformation demands the ongoing observation and exploration of your patterns of perception.

The higher mind is the discerning aspect you use to look within and pierce through a distorted perception to access the peace, love, and happiness you naturally crave. Self-reflection leads to a deeper understanding of yourself and others, inciting the desire for something more real that eventually prompts you to seek what lies beyond your ordinary ego consciousness. Discriminative wisdom is a path to liberation. At this mental level, however, your ego easily becomes "spiritualized" or fixated on mere intellectual knowledge to remain in control of your perception and behavior.

Remember that the legitimate function of the mind is to show you *everything you are not*, through your observation and awareness, so that you may peel away the veils of ignorance that keep you from realizing the truth of who you are.

THE CAUSAL BODY

The causal body is known as the subconscious, or the repository of memories, desires, and instinctual or involuntary physiological processes. It is the first sheath wrapping the Inner Self (or Spirit) at the core of your soul. As the site of your intuitive senses and the pure joy of your original nature, it is also known as the *spiritual body* or *bliss body*, because it leads to the recognition of your divinity through superconscious or mystical states. Like the different levels of a river, the surface is your conscious mind, the underlying currents carry your subconscious patterns of perception, and the riverbed supporting and directing it all is the absolute reality of the Self.

This layer is called *causal body* because it holds, in seed form, the impressions, tendencies, desires, and karma from previous experiences that *cause* specific situations in your reality and shape your perception of it. Your identification with the mind urges you to find either logical or supernatural explanations for certain events and people in your life, but in reality, it all comes down to which causal seeds (or *samskaras*) are predominant and active, which ones remain dormant, and which ones you continue cultivating or you put to sleep.

When similar thoughts and experiences accumulate, they turn into positive, negative, or mixed tendencies and subliminal traits that produce unconscious impulses toward the same type of thoughts and actions. Just like a tree grows from a seed and yields seeds of re-creation, the imprints of past experiences generate similar types of experiences, which in turn leave more impressions that reinforce the tendency toward those experiences.

This mental loop results from the revolving quality of the mind constantly churning thoughts, which I will explore in more detail later on. It makes breaking addictions or negative habits difficult, but it can also solidify positive ones. You are here to heal painful subconscious tendencies while fulfilling your innate drive for expression and freedom. Everything you need to undergo and learn is already within you, in potential form, which is why it is crucial to know yourself to transcend your suffering.

The causal body is where the creative power of Consciousness arises, which, in absolute terms, can be viewed as the ignorance or darkness that veils the pure light of the Self with its many manifestations. Without this veil of ignorance, there is no soul or mind or ego or body, and therefore no individualized reality. The ego-mind cannot know itself, so it makes you view the subconscious as a dangerous underworld, because it contains the false ideas and beliefs through which the Self identifies with the mind to experience the material world. This, along with your attachment to sensory perception, creates great resistance to look within, to remove the root of your afflictions.

Beyond the subconscious lies the superconscious, or the intelligence that transcends the mind. You may access it in various stages, such as: vivid dreaming; dreamless yogic sleep; glimpses into subtle or ethereal realms; states of pure stillness; states of cosmic consciousness (the Inner Witness or Inner Self); states of God consciousness or ecstatic devotion and bliss; and states of Universal Awareness or non-duality in the Supreme Self. These subtle dimensions of yourself become real as you pierce through the mental layers; they emerge from the causal seeds or imprints of introspection, spiritual practices, and mystical experiences in this and previous lifetimes.

Feelings of joy, gratitude, and peace arise from this aspect as well. If the mind is still, because of spiritual discipline or Grace, a state of pure bliss arises. Bliss is not a sensory emotion; it is profound happiness without a reason—the ecstasy of simply *being*, connected to the totality of life in the ego-less-ness of the spiritual heart. It is a taste of your true Self—the pure love that removes all divisions—and it can range from desireless joy to a mystical, childlike openness beyond the mental realms. But the ego can also use those types of experiences to become spiritualized and increase its self-importance. This is why some people may have flashes of illumination, be highly intuitive, or have psychic powers yet remain spiritually immature, lacking mental discipline and self-awareness. Spiritual powers do not lead to the Self; they become a distraction when you fixate on them.

Because of the fluctuations of the ego-mind, moments of bliss tend to be temporary, but they can also turn more permanent through intense devotion or steady meditative states where the "experiencer" disappears, along with ideas like, "This is *me*, this is *my* experience." A superconscious state is known as *samadhi* or *nirvana*. In the West, it has been described as the *mystical union* with God, which results from completely surrendering to Divine Will.

Samadhi means "sameness, oneness, or union" with the object of meditation. It is the total absorption in that object, when the ego consciousness disappears. In this sense, it is the emptiness of mind that brings inner peace and leads to spiritual enlightenment through various stages, such as *nirvikalpa, asamprajnata,* or *sasmita samadhi* ("superconsciousness without imagination, without seeds, or with full knowledge of pure *I-am-ness*"). Advaita Vedanta speaks of *sahaja samadhi* as our "original" or "natural" state of Pure Awareness, which is a kind of neutral bliss as well, and of *turiya*, or the "fourth state," similar to deep, dreamless sleep but with the consciousness of the wakeful state.

You reclaim it through the effort to keep the mind still, going beyond your identifications with sensory perception and piercing through all the energy layers of your soul, because they maintain the illusion of separation as well. Spiritual maturity can be gauged by how long you are able to remain in a state of *no-mind*, excluding all unwanted thoughts by refusing to follow them or by concentrating on a single thought; this is how the ego-mind is restrained and gradually dissolves. However, the lower levels of superconscious states can make someone believe they have reached enlightenment or have been chosen by God to lead others, even though they're strongly attached to their sensory perception and desires.

Unaware of their delusion, they simply strengthen their ego with spiritual knowledge or powers, which is quite common nowadays as we go through a universal cycle known as *Kali Yuga*. It is a spiritual Dark Age where life revolves mostly around sensual gratification, money, and power, because Consciousness is diminished while the ego is magnified. It brims with false teachers, self-proclaimed prophets and gurus, and all kinds of cults and cult-like behaviors.

Cult leaders and false gurus are hard to recognize, since they use aspects of the truth while distorting it to their advantage to hide their real intentions. Even your attachment to the physical form of a real, *bona fide* guru can hinder your spiritual development. A true master shows you the path to the teacher within, which is your true Self, without any self-interest or dogmatic rules. But it is your responsibility to tend to your unconscious, wounded needs to remain free from manipulation and power dynamics, and find the way back to yourself.

The ultimate goal of life is uncovering your divine nature by breaking free from all the beliefs and concepts binding you to the world of appearances or impermanent forms. Raising your awareness beyond the bliss body entails renouncing *all* the worldly entrapments of your ego. Spiritual practices like meditation, mantra, prayer, chanting, self-inquiry, selfless service, and the study of sacred texts, as well as the teachings of enlightened masters, are powerful tools to achieve this. But they are tools; they can liberate you through your own effort, or they can keep you in delusion if your ego uses them to feel superior or create more attachments.

Furthermore, when you commit to a daily spiritual discipline to purify the mind, negative impressions and tendencies will surface and get in your way. These burn out with humility and devotion, or through self-knowledge—that is, the investigation of your ego-mind. By cultivating self-awareness and love, you can dismiss the negative thoughts, patterns, and tendencies that distort your perception, thus healing the karmic dynamics that trap you in low, painful levels of existence. This is how you transform your experience of reality from within.

***

Soham-Hamsa Pranayama

This is a breathing practice to help you relax and quiet the mind. Try to do a few rounds every day before the Developing Stillness exercise from the previous chapter and whenever you feel restless. Sit in a comfortable position where you will not be interrupted, and practice for at least ten to fifteen minutes.

Block your right nostril as you breathe in through the left nostril while mentally saying the mantra *So*. Then block the left nostril as you breathe out through the right nostril with the mantra *Ham*. Reverse the process immediately, inhaling through the right nostril with the mantra *Ham*, then block it to exhale through the left nostril with *Sa*. Again, breathe in through the left nostril with *So*, then block it to breathe out through the right nostril with *Ham*. Continue like this, alternating your inhalations and exhalations with *So … Ham … Ham … Sa … So … Ham … Ham … Sa …* Make your breathing slow and smooth, until your mind quiets down.

Soham and *Hamsa* (its reverse) are the natural sounds of your breath. They can be translated as "I am That" (the Supreme Self). *Soham* is the feminine, lunar aspect of your breathing, which is cooling, while *Hamsa* is the solar, masculine, heating aspect. When you alternate them, you increase and balance prana by unifying these polar energies within you.

This exercise strengthens the lungs and digestion and increases prana, while improving concentration and memory. If you practice regularly, it will turn into a spontaneous response when you get anxious or triggered.

THE REVELATION:

A DIVINE PLAY

CHAPTER THREE

The Karmic Unfolding of Reality

You are what your deep, driving desire is. As your desire is, so is your will. As your will is, so is your deed. As your deed is, so is your destiny.

— *Brihadaranyaka Upanishad*

After breaking into a rich house and stealing as many valuables as they could carry, a couple of thieves rushed back to their hiding spot. Once they felt safe, the oldest of the two handed some money to his partner, saying, "I am famished. Go get some food before we split our goods."

The young man agreed and headed to the marketplace. As he was pondering what he would do with his share of the loot, a sudden idea popped into his mind. "Wait a minute. If I kill the old guy, I won't have to share anything, and I can keep the whole thing to myself!" After purchasing some food and rat poison, he gobbled up his portion and then mixed the poison into the rest of the food before walking back, feeling excited about the future.

Meanwhile, his associate was entertaining similar ideas while he admired the stolen treasure. "When that kid comes through the door," he thought, "I'll stab him to death so I won't have to share the fruits of *my* work!" As planned, when the younger burglar arrived, he welcomed him with a sharp knife until the victim fell to the ground and died. Then he washed his hands and weapon before proceeding to eat his meal with great gusto, only to succumb to his death next to his partner in crime.

The ego-mind is inherently greedy. It craves more pleasure, more stuff, more recognition, more control, and more power to experience a momentary gratification that hides the sense of deficiency it also produces by blocking Consciousness. The external world is a creation of the ego-mind, and it is ruled by it. You need this ego consciousness to act and express yourself out there, but it also makes you believe that you will find happiness in what the world has to offer. However, as you engage with it, you get attached to things and people that are invariably bound to change, which causes you suffering.

Since the world is a creation of the ego that is ruled and experienced by the ego, suffering happens only in the ego-mind as a result of your identification with the physical body that makes you feel like a separate person. In this sense, your pain is both inevitable and necessary, because your distress and discontentment eventually lead you to seek something more real than the fleeting enjoyment of the senses. To put it simply, pleasure puts you to sleep and pain wakes you up!

Pleasurable situations bring about a desire for more pleasure, and painful events leave mental imprints of fear and an aversion to certain experiences, people, and things. The more energy and time you invest in the object of any desire, the more attached you become; and the tighter you hold on, the fear of losing it also increases, which makes you cling even more.

This turns into a vicious cycle that disconnects you from the freedom and peace of your essential nature, forming energy knots and patterns you keep reinforcing with more attachments

The Karmic Unfolding of Reality

and negative emotions that block the flow of Consciousness within. When self-awareness is missing or weak, the process usually goes like this:

1. Your ego-mind produces a desire, along with the expectation of its fulfillment, which creates an attachment to the object of your desire.
2. If it is obstructed or jeopardized in any way, the fear of not acquiring or of losing the object of your desire turns into anger, which is a mechanism of the ego to protect itself from its own limitations.
3. Anger disconnects you from your spiritual heart, creating a sense of isolation that further accentuates the separation from the object of your desire.
4. This disconnection allows confusion and ignorance to take over your perception, instigating impulsive actions to fulfill your desire while blurring the clarity to see the potential consequences of your choices.

If suppressed or unresolved, anger is either directed within and turns into depression or physical issues, or it may show up when you least expect it. It is like being trapped in a cage where nothing matters but your desire and the emotions that go with it. The more intense the desire, the stronger the entrapment and the longer it takes to realize you hold the key to escape your own mental cage. Clearly, there is a big difference between the impulse to argue when you find opposition and that of killing someone because you feel entitled to what they have, as in my story of the two thieves. But both types of situations are directed by the self-centeredness of the ego, only with different degrees of ignorance and hostility.

Desires are very powerful; they move you forward through your goals and take you on your human adventure from one experience (or lifetime) to the next. When discrimination is weak or missing, the ongoing flow of desires and fears produced by the ego obstructs the capacity to discern what is real or imaginary and what leads to happiness or suffering. In my story above, greed overpowers everything else, leading both thieves to their destruction. It is a symbolic example of the workings of the ego and the mechanisms it creates to hide the negative tendencies that start the cycle from desire to destructive action in the first place. This is why people find all kinds of justifications for their destructive choices when they are blinded by selfish motivations.

But because they go against your true nature, harmful actions leave impressions that produce unconscious guilt, which is like a wound that pinches you out of the flow of life in both obvious and subtle ways, eventually causing difficulties and toxic dynamics with yourself and others. This happens whether a desire hurts another being, a group, a community, a country, or yourself, although the effects will be different. The more power anyone holds, at any level, the greater their responsibility not to cause harm and the more intense the repercussions of doing so. Conscious or unconscious, a hostile action is motivated by ego and leaves causal seeds that in time will bring suffering.

As long as you identify with the ego-mind, your journey through the dreamworld is governed by the Law of Karma, which weaves your reality with both pleasant and painful experiences as a result of previous choices. In Sanskrit, *karma* means "action" or "deed," so this law operates through the egoic sense of doership and ownership that sustains the delusion of duality. Truly, all actions emerge in Consciousness, from the Self and for the Self, and just like you are not actually affected by the actions in your dreams, the Self is a neutral witness to the actions in the cosmic dream and is never affected by them.

Karma exists in the ego, for the ego—through the perception of individualized experience that makes you think, "This is *my* will, *my* intention, *my* action." You renounce your actions and their outcomes when you completely surrender your ego, but until you get there, you are solely responsible for all of them, to gain self-awareness as you experience their consequences. Anything that you think you own or do is impermanent and can be taken away from you in an instant. But if you remove your identifications and attachments, acting like a humble vessel of Consciousness in the play of Consciousness, then who is performing those actions and who is to suffer the painful results of previous actions? Once you achieve full spiritual freedom, you stop creating karma and any past karma works itself out spontaneously, without you having to do anything, since the *doer* disappears.

The Law of Karma has been perceived as a law of cause-and-effect conveying some type of punishment or payback, but karmic dynamics can be as complex and multilayered as each individual soul, shaped by a variety of events along its convoluted journey of evolution and involution. Your path appears linear—as past, present, and future—because the mind conceptualizes change as time and space with the idea of continuity. But Consciousness is not linear; it encompasses everything at once. Many factors play a part in the outcome of a single action, and its ripple effects may extend and change in unforeseen ways.

A tree develops from a seed, but to undergo such transformation, the seed requires the right soil to grow roots and the right temperature to sprout, in addition to receiving enough sunshine, water, and nutrients to continue expanding. Without these, nothing will grow out of that seed. If it has to compete for light, or if it finds obstacles along the way, rather than blossoming into a strong, straight tree, it may have to bend to get the light and space it needs. All of these conditions result from the elements and qualities of nature combining in certain ways. A famous scientist once said that if you want to make an apple pie from scratch, you must first invent the universe. Indeed, the whole universe is involved in any action or outcome, because you are your own universe; nothing exists in isolation, only the ego creates this illusion by dividing and separating things.

Your soul is a self-directed spark of light traveling a unique path of maturity in resonance with karmic conditions you cannot control. In addition, it fulfills a function for other souls to play out their karma as well. It may be difficult to understand why certain people and situations appear or disappear from your life; why those you love reject or turn their back on you; or why you have to bear lack and limitations on some level when other people seem to get what they (or you) want. Now, if the ultimate goal of your journey is to awaken from the collective dream, how do you know that positive conditions are better than the seemingly negative conditions that prod you to seek spiritual freedom? You cannot foresee where any given situation will lead you, but you can trust that it is meant to happen as it happens for your own growth—as the unfolding of Consciousness through your body and mind.

People get confused when they are told they chose their parents and circumstances before incarnating. How could they have chosen to be neglected or abused, to lose a child or a spouse, or to live with sickness or financial problems, when all they want is to be happy? Indeed, the idea of your life being a willful *choice* or some kind of "contract" doesn't make any sense, especially if you comprehend that life is a play of Consciousness orchestrated by the eternal Self to experience itself. Besides, how could you have chosen your circumstances when even now you are hardly aware of the real motivations behind your reactions? To make conscious choices, you need to know yourself, which is what painful situations prompt you to do: to look within.

Your soul transmigrates through desire and *resonance*. When the physical body dies, it carries in the causal body memories of past actions, experiences, and unresolved desires in seed form. These draw your soul to continue its human adventure, although it may also go to other planes along its journey. Your parents, family, social environment, culture, relationships, and the main events in your life result from these causal seeds as well. Each incarnation unfolds in perfect synchronicity with everyone and everything else, although not necessarily as a linear process, so you may have to suffer the consequences of past actions performed within a very different set of circumstances.

Furthermore, your soul is like a cell in a cosmic organism, self-directed to fulfill its function within the collective dreamworld. Your individual road map is shaped through the qualities of nature according to your past karma and mental patterns, but it also responds to the needs of the cosmic organism as a whole. You have no control over any of this, so it makes no sense to think you were a terrible person in the past if you find challenging or distressing situations. Even the idea of being the same person throughout your soul journey is an illusion. You identify with the body you were born into, but you are the eternal Self that is never born and never dies.

As an expression of Consciousness, you carry the seeds of both karma (past) and destiny (future), but you cannot be truly free while you are trapped between them. Only the present is real. What matters is what you do to transform the distorted perception that causes your suffering *now*. This is your spiritual responsibility, and your reality offers everything you need to leave the past behind by uncovering the meaning of your life.

Actions that have been repeated many times become active, primary tendencies of perception and behavior, while other inclinations may be latent or secondary. Predominant karma brings forth your species, life span, and main circumstances, while secondary karma either supports the primary one, is destroyed without fruition, or remains dormant for a number of births. Since your soul is trapped in a sensory body to undergo its human experience, this plane of experience entails physical and mental pain. Suffering has intensified in these dark times of exacerbated egoism, but, at the same time, the density of a highly materialistic world offers many opportunities for karmic resolution; you are burning negative karma simply by being here in this time and age.

Pain is meant to help you dissolve the delusion of duality that causes it. The Self is Pure Consciousness, while the ego-mind is completely unconscious; as the aspect that blocks Awareness, it cannot be aware of itself. The mind is the screen reflecting the light that makes everything apparent, and the ego gets in the way of the light to individualize people and objects like the shadows in a shadow play. The shadows aren't real, but you believe them to be real, so you either resist or get attached to them, getting increasingly entangled with the world of appearances. This causes you suffering until you dissolve your own shadows by directing the light of Awareness toward them, which makes the ego and the pain disappear as well.

Although unreal, the ego creates the sense of experience you perceive as *your* circumstances and *your* pain until you surrender this burden of doership and ownership that produces sorrow. Like a caged bird, you get used to your prison while trying to make it more pleasant and comfortable, but the yearning for true freedom and happiness never disappears; these are your inherent, essential aspects, even if the ego-mind distorts them time and time again. They are the real driving forces behind all your desires and actions.

Negative karma results from selfish deeds, while positive karma comes from generous, loving choices. Acts of kindness and selfless service balance negative karmic dynamics through a deep, subconscious sense of unity—the intuitive wisdom that we are all different expressions of the One eternal Self sharing the suffering of the same egoic delusion. We have all taken the roles of victims and perpetrators, saintly and sinful, selfish and unselfish, rich and poor, powerful and powerless; we have also alternated genders, races, and cultural origins through countless incarnations to explore the full spectrum of human experience.

Any act that goes against Consciousness creates a wound in the person performing it and the one enduring it. You can think of this wound as a debt of love and light. It creates suffering in the recipient while pinching the one causing it out of the flow of life, becoming subconscious fear and guilt that binds both souls (through resonance) to either repeat or heal the lack of love. The more intense or forceful an act, the deeper the imprints it leaves; and the more it is repeated, the stronger the impulse to repeat it becomes. These tendencies drive the soul to reincarnate again and again in search of resolution and healing.

One of my teachers used to say that in a very few people, the ego is like paper that burns quickly; in others, it is like wood that burns slowly; and in some folks, it is like a rock that takes a very long time to disintegrate. The ego is fundamentally self-centered, mostly dominated by ignorance and egoism. If reinforced, egoism can become what is known as narcissism. A narcissist hides behind a false, magnified self-image to protect a deep sense of disconnection from themselves. Their ego blocks all empathy and real connection with others to avoid feeling vulnerable, because their main motivation is the illusion of control through the gratification of selfish or hostile desires. This may give way to psychopathic or sociopathic behaviors if the perception is overpowered by hatred and destructive tendencies.

These are extreme degrees of ego entrapment that fixate the mind on the need to control another person, a group, a community, or a country for the satisfaction of unconscious urges. The main drive of a narcissist is the desire for external power to compensate for a lack of true power, which is love. However, the very nature of ego is the self-centeredness that creates power dynamics, so everyone has the egoic impulse to control life in some way. It just varies in intensity, depending on the predominant tendencies of perception at play.

There is a tug-of-war between Divine Consciousness at the core of your soul and the ego-mind pushing thoughts and desires to maintain the delusion of duality through codependent power dynamics. Previous negative choices left causal seeds that may blossom into unpleasant situations through the negative habits of thought that now color your attitudes and experiences. You are here to resolve them as you harvest your investments of energy in the karmic pool of debts and merits through your own distorted perception.

Past karma determines your genetic information, physical appearance, gender, family, and cultural environment, as well as your circumstances and main life events. Present karma corresponds to the actions you take in your current life that yield short-term consequences. You create future karma when you are unable to rectify past and present karma before the end of a lifetime; its imprints remain in the causal body to be addressed in the future.

All karma is exhausted through karma. Negative actions are balanced with ego-less deeds, not actions that appear to be good but are really self-serving. Beyond the external appearances, every choice either leads you toward or away from your true Self. In addition, your individual karma also unfolds in connection to your family, culture, country, and the groups to which you belong, as well as humanity as a whole. Karma is always collective, because it invariably involves and affects other people; plus, we are all connected at a subconscious level, so our actions create ripple effects passed down from one person to another and one generation to the next. No wonder why we witness so much suffering and imbalance in the world!

Negative karmic dynamics often start with a deviation from the truth—either hiding it from yourself or from others. When you dismiss your inner voice, cover up selfish motivations, or lie about something out of fear, guilt, or greed, your disconnection produces a fertile mental terrain for negative causal seeds to sprout. Sometimes you may be able to counter the deviation from the truth right away, and other times you further disconnect from yourself with more lies or deceit, until you lose track of the truth and fall into destructive actions.

If you throw a pebble up in the air, you may be able to catch it before it hits the ground. Likewise, some negative karma may be corrected right away with conscious actions or a self-imposed sacrifice. If you harm someone, willingly or unwillingly, you can try to make amends to ease their pain and your disconnection. However, certain actions require more time, energy, or suffering to restore balance. For instance, murder and rape cannot be cancelled out because they cannot be undone and go against the very purpose of life. Their ripple effects affect many souls, in the moment and in the future, leaving deep individual and collective imprints of powerlessness, hatred, and guilt.

And yet, since it is all a dream or play of Consciousness, the suffering in the world will resolve in its own time. You may feel guided to contribute positive actions along your human adventure, directing your energy toward awareness and kindness, but your greatest gift will always be your own transformation. Healing your distorted perception has a profound impact on how the world appears to you, because you are the Awareness that makes it real. Your choices determine whether you remain trapped in the suffering of the ego-mind or you awaken from the collective delusion. If you want peace and love in the world, you must cultivate those in yourself to see them reflected on the outside.

Until your mind is completely purified, your causal seeds shape the course of current and future experiences. You carry the seeds left by every impression and action throughout your soul journey. Your desires and habits of thought have produced ingrained inclinations as well. Imagine how many seeds lie within you, each with the potential to blossom and reinforce old patterns of perception, if given the right terrain. This is why certain people may trigger strong feelings of attraction or aversion, or awaken the best or the worst in you.

You are an appearance of Consciousness on an individualized adventure, and so is everyone else. How you perceive, interpret, and react to life is unique, even if you share beliefs and experiences with others. It is important to recognize that your mental patterns can be nurtured or put to sleep, but they cannot be destroyed with psychological work alone. Because they actualize in the mind, they can only vanish beyond the mind, in the light of superconscious states, profound devotion, or the earnest investigation of the ego to dissolve it in its source. That is, in the radiance of Pure Awareness or the absolute surrender to God.

Positive karma brings auspicious situations and opportunities while negative karma weaves your life path with difficult circumstances and events that make you feel trapped. They help you atone for previous actions and attitudes that reflect a disconnect from your divine nature. No one escapes this, so even if it looks like someone is getting away with destructive acts, at some point they will suffer limitations and pain to prod them back toward love. This is the nature and the destination of all souls.

People may deceive others, conceal their crimes, and lie to themselves to justify their wrongdoings, but nobody can hide the imprints that selfish deeds leave in their subconscious. In time, these will manifest in some way to bring about balance. Your main concern, however, should be healing the distorted perception that bring *you* pain, trusting that everything happens as it is meant to happen within the cosmic dream. You don't need to understand or "fix" everything.

Although the ego-mind produces ideas of justice, injustice, punishment, and revenge, it is essential to comprehend that this is a cosmic play where the eternal Self goes on a scavenger hunt for all sorts of experiences and eventually finds the way back to itself. In other words, at some point the sorrow inherent in worldly desires leads all human beings to yearn for inner peace. The Law of Karma is not about punishment or retaliation, and there is nobody out there pulling the strings for you to go through difficult situations. This is a play of Consciousness unfolding in your mind, nudging you to mature and awaken from your own dream. In other words, it is all appearances of Consciousness making you conscious of yourself until you realize that you are Consciousness.

To stop feeding negative tendencies and accumulating energetic debts, you have to accept your suffering and restrictions but without identifying with them or feeling like a victim. As the mystic poet Rumi put it, *the cure for pain is in the pain*. You find the way out of sorrow by surrendering your ego to something bigger, something more stable or permanent. Everything in your personal dream is already set for you. In reality, it is all directed by the Self for the Self through the many appearances it takes through the play of the *gunas* in your mind.

Now, if your life is just an illusion shaped by the qualities of nature, do actions really matter? The paradoxical essence of Consciousness is at play here. In a sense, nothing you do matters, because things happen the way they are meant to happen, without ever affecting the Self that imagines them. At the same time, everything you do matters, because your attitudes and reactions determine the nature of your experiences. You are responsible for them, since they are what you can actually change; your choices either keep you ensnared in the cosmic dream or liberate you from it.

The path to freedom demands taking spiritual responsibility for everything in your reality, accepting things and people as they are, not just the aspects you enjoy but also those that aren't pleasant, with the understanding that any distress comes from your own resistance to life, which is fluid and changeable. By developing self-awareness and humility, you can see any difficult situation as a divine gift nudging you to remove the illusions that cause you suffering. You cannot transcend your pain without accepting the limitations of your ego consciousness. This is a gradual process that can be equated to climbing up a pyramid, which I call the *Love-Consciousness Pyramid*.

At the lower levels, where most people experience life, there is a complete identification with the physical body, and therefore with the ego-mind. Every soul moves up to higher levels as it develops devotion or self-awareness through the many experiences it undergoes between pleasure and pain. Naturally, due to the deceptive quality of the ego, the number of individuals following this direction diminishes considerably at every stage, so it takes a very long time to reach the top. There are just a few highly evolved beings who achieve full enlightenment at any given time, as a result of their effort over many lifetimes.

The Love-Consciousness Pyramid

My illustration displays possible attributes and stages of karma, experience, and awareness, representing the soul journey as a whole, as well as during each incarnation. The qualities along the Pyramid refer to the mental-emotional states through this process. They are not fixed and can be interpreted from various levels of perception—as different lifetimes or the stages within each birth, including your current one. The purpose here is to give you an idea of the road map toward spiritual maturity.

SELF

SPIRITUAL FREEDOM
- Love
- Devotion
- Surrender

INNER PEACE
- Humility
- Kindness
- Forgiveness
- Self-Awareness

DISPASSION
- Responsibility
- Non-attachment
- Empathy Compassion
- Intelligence Knowledge

AWARENESS
- Judgment Arrogance
- Fear Guilt Envy Selfishness
- Depression Compulsions
- Egoism Power Anger Cruelty

CONTROL
- Ignorance Jealousy Revenge
- Addictions Manipulation Deceit
- Lust Instinctual Urges Base Desires
- Greed Hatred Violence Destruction

SUFFERING

EGO

The snake symbolizes the *Kundalini Shakti*, the Feminine creative principle of Divine Consciousness or the Self (also known as *Maya*) that brings into existence the illusion of the physical realm. It is considered the chief prana or vital force from which all other energies and the ego arise. It remains dormant while the soul is busy pursuing worldly desires and then gradually clears the path to Self-realization. Its upward journey represents the maturity needed to get to the top of the Pyramid, because the natural direction of the ego-mind is toward lower, negative tendencies that block but may also overlap with positive ones. It is not unusual to feel like you are taking one step forward and three steps back, since ordinary consciousness fluctuates as you engage with the world.

There is no self-awareness at the very bottom, where the most destructive tendencies predominate. This is where base passions such as greed, lust, jealousy, arrogance, anger, and hatred rule the mind, leading to violent behavior, either hidden or overt, as well as the impulse to lie, steal, cheat, abuse, exploit, and kill. The entrapment of ego is so strong that there is no empathy or discrimination. Complete ignorance of the Inner Self yields the fantasy that only sensual pleasure, money, and power bring happiness, thus becoming the main driving forces in life.

Because of the stronghold of sensory perception, it is clear that this illusion pervades the external world, through a constant craving for experiences, but those at the bottom of the Pyramid cannot see any purpose beyond the satisfaction of base urges. Chasing instant gratification and control, they refuse to accept any obstacles or losses while deflecting any responsibility for their choices. This reinforces their hostile tendencies and internal turmoil, since they are unable to see their actions objectively; they are totally trapped in the self-centeredness of the ego-mind. Such behavior promotes toxic karmic dynamics that tend to repeat over many births, in a vicious circle of painful, traumatic upbringings and harmful habits.

You are no longer at the bottom of the Pyramid, or you wouldn't be reading this book; but situations that trigger intense anger, jealousy, or passion can bring you here, even if momentarily, as you continue seeking sensory experiences. Hard drugs and excess alcohol may do this as well, for they block the discrimination of the higher mind. Also, any negative emotion with which you identify can pull you down at any moment, if you stop seeing yourself or others with compassion. You may not actually steal from or kill another person, but you can sabotage your relationships or your dreams with negative tendencies that obstruct the flow of life, thus letting the ego-mind kill your joy and enthusiasm to the point of despair, depression, or self-harm.

Selfish motivations remain strong above the lowest level, and only what is tangible and measurable is deemed real, although the desire to find a way out of suffering may have been aroused. It often develops, however, into the need to control people with guilt, fear, anger, and other forms of manipulation. Relationships turn into power struggles through a mutual projection of shortcomings and weaknesses. Here the illusion of control is strengthened by rationalizing uncomfortable feelings and hiding any insecurities behind judgments and complaints.

The prevailing self-centeredness of the ego produces the idea that other people should meet our needs and desires to make our life easier. Through the difficulties we encounter, we gradually realize that the world does not revolve around us, and we try to avoid conflicts. Because of the isolating nature of the ego, we get upset or feel like victims when our expectations aren't met. We compare ourselves to and envy others, placing them above or below us; this may prompt us to lie, cheat, manipulate, or fight to get what we want. The delusion of duality is too strong to see that by hurting others, even if in our imagination, we are hurting ourselves.

Our perception and actions may reflect rigid religious views from our upbringing (or previous incarnations), which we either disguise or feel compelled to impose on others. If there is no religious taint, similar power dynamics may take a more rational, intellectual, metaphysical, or even magical coloring. The spiritual dimension of life is perceived as the polarity of "good" against "evil" found in religions, cults, and metaphysical groups, which simply reflects the power dynamics created by the delusion of duality. This can also be expressed as an attraction to lower spirits, ghosts, aliens, and extrasensory perception, or to artificial states beyond ordinary consciousness with mind-altering or psychedelic substances.

Most people join a church or group of like-minded peers to gain a sense of belonging and purpose. The idea of changing the world, creating a collective heaven, or achieving some kind of mass redemption or spiritual ascension may sound appealing, because the thought of being freer than others stirs up too much guilt, while, at the same time, making everyone involved feel special. It is a great trick of the ego that veils the possibility to conceive life beyond duality—the *otherness* of family, friends, and those with whom we share beliefs and experiences.

On a more personal level, you judge harshly those who appear to be different, especially if they question what makes you feel safe. You think you are "right" and others are "wrong." There is no real awareness of how the ego-mind controls your perception, so any unpleasant feelings prompt you to blame other people rather than observing your own negative attitudes and tendencies. You try to keep up the appearances—the self-images you work hard to build and protect—and only let your barriers down under the effect of alcohol and other drugs.

You move up the Love-Consciousness Pyramid by gradually taking responsibility for your perception and behavior. You continue seeking happiness and pleasure, but now you begin to see the consequences of your actions. The unraveling of past and present karma fuels your craving for peace and love, although you believe you will find them outside of you. You fixate on the people you are attached to, creating expectations that bring disappointment. You are becoming more conscientious of others and would like to share yourself, but your unconscious, wounded needs make you defensive or push you to shut down when others don't respond the way you want.

That is, you are mostly *reactive*. You complain, argue, or try to control those around you when you feel misunderstood or unappreciated. You also suffer if your self-images and ideas about life are challenged. In time, however, you recognize that impulsive reactions cause conflicts, so you try to establish less painful interactions. You want to find your place in the world and experience a sense of partnership and community, so you start developing tolerance and flexibility while being more open and generous as well. But you expect the same in return, which keeps you spinning in power dynamics and blame games fueled by illusions and resentment.

You may seek emotional or spiritual support at some point. Your desire for clarity is increasing, so you try to find ways to gain deeper insight into your life. This builds momentum to move up the Love-Consciousness Pyramid. If you continue with this process, you uncover your hidden motivations and become more aware of the part you play in your interactions, although you still hold others responsible for your pain and feel responsible for theirs. You focus on work and relationships, but there is a nagging feeling that something is missing. You may already have what you thought would make you happy, yet you cannot seem to find fulfillment.

If your desire for clarity intensifies, your efforts may activate positive soul memories and causal seeds from previous births. Now you are more empathetic and sensitive to the suffering on the planet, and you want to help others in some way. This provides a strong sense of purpose that makes you feel good. Then you start including yourself in this equation of love, establishing self-care routines and practices like yoga, meditation, martial arts, and so on. If self-awareness increases, you begin discovering deeper dimensions of yourself. Your intuitive senses also increase, or you feel a desire to develop them. As you trust a non-cognitive perception, you may suddenly awaken to the Divine or to a new vision of life.

A deeper understanding may dawn on you or result from painful events. You seek guidance, information, and like-minded people to support your new perspective and feel empowered in a community (even if virtual) with which to share your views. Although mental fluctuations and painful impressions continue to dominate your perception, feeling that you are not alone brings reassurance to balance out your doubts. You are gaining an intellectual comprehension of the truth, but the experience of it is missing or comes as fleeting insights.

As you move forward, your ego-mind triggers great resistance, disrupting your progress at every opportunity. It clouds your perception by becoming spiritualized, making you feel special or superior. You want to share your knowledge, maybe help others as well, but this desire most likely comes from a wounded need for validation that distracts you from delving more deeply within to continue moving up the Pyramid. Perhaps you try to convince family members and friends of what they may not be ready to see or accept, so you end up feeling alone while judging them for their ignorance. It is not unusual at this stage to have the desire to renounce the world by moving to a monastery or ashram, although it may be just another way to avoid dealing with the painful reality of your own karma.

If the ego-mind remains in control of your behavior, your reactions pull your energy to lower levels of consciousness. You may try to rise above by reading books and taking workshops or courses to develop spiritually, but there is a misalignment between your new understanding, your emotions, and your reality. You are still reactive and feel pulled in different directions, swinging between your unconscious impulses and the higher principles you want to follow but haven't yet actualized. You want to express yourself freely, but how you think other people perceive you is still more important than your own freedom. At this point, personal or group dynamics may stir up deeper issues you try to avoid by keeping busy or distracted.

You go from insight and love to self-consciousness and fear; from peace and contentment to anger and judgment; from excitement and hope to anxiety and lack of enthusiasm, and everything in between. The ego has a polarizing effect that brings you up and down the Love-Consciousness Pyramid for a long while. You are more in touch with yourself, discovering and releasing some of your negative aspects, but you often doubt the process and may want to quit your self-exploration when it brings about uncomfortable feelings. There is an ominous sense that something bad will happen if you continue delving within; that you will lose the people and things you are attached to; that your life will make no sense without the perception with which you are comfortable and familiar; or that you are never going to achieve the freedom you yearn for.

The ego-mind creates resistance by directing your attention to the outside, mainly keeping it on *others*. If you don't have the support of a group or community, you may consult psychics, mediums, and the like to gain a sense of control about the future because you are scared to be fully present in life. Again, it is crucial to pierce through your resistance with discipline and self-awareness, surrendering your ego at every step. Without a real, *bona fide* teacher, a steady spiritual practice, or an effective system to know and master the mind, your mental-emotional states will continue wavering between clarity and confusion as you engage with the world.

Here is a simple analogy of your path. Imagine you are in a rowboat in the middle of the ocean. Everywhere you look, all you see is endless water, but you keep rowing and rowing. Although you are getting better at it, your undertaking often seems pointless; it takes much effort and there are no signs telling you if you are any closer to your destination. In fact, you don't even know what your destination looks like! You may have some ideas, but there are no landmarks guiding you or any indication of where you are, only sporadic insights that keep you going.

At this point, which occurs many, many times on the path to spiritual freedom, it is essential to remain committed. If you rebel against your process or the unfolding of your life, the currents of your ego will take you on a detour, making your journey longer. You may also stagnate where you are, either believing you have made it to your destination, disbelieving you will ever make it, or spinning in the intellectual understanding of the truth that provides an illusion of control but no true peace or freedom.

If you remain determined, however, you can embrace the uncertainty of the ego-mind and may find real guidance, often as a result of previous positive actions and a shift in your perception. When you stop hiding from yourself, recognizing that your afflictions and difficulties stem from the choices you have made and keep making, in due course you relinquish the need to fight or fix life, and stop trying to meet some absurd ideal of perfection that keeps you enslaved to your ego. Only your earnest, increasing yearning fuels a renewed sense of purpose. Once you perceive your life as an adventure of self-discovery, your spiritual journey truly begins!

As you continue gaining self-awareness, you dwell less on negative emotions, even if you still react to other people's opinions and behaviors, because you are able to see yourself and others more clearly. Now you can catch yourself trying to avoid unpleasant feelings and are more open to accepting them. You observe your thoughts and emotions as well as the tendency to judge yourself and others, and you start questioning the motivations behind them. You are becoming more mindful and present, comprehending that your reality arises from within you.

At higher levels, personal and spiritual growth becomes a priority, and the longing for the Divine intensifies. Now you understand that everything is determined by karma, accepting that you have no control over life and that you don't need to control it either. Fear and doubt may creep in whenever a deep desire or attachment is challenged, but you are willing to let go, being more surrendered and at peace. Worldly entrapments are becoming less appealing as well; you know the enjoyment they bring is too temporary. Your worldly responsibilities no longer feel like burdens, and you engage with greater detachment and curiosity, viewing your daily experiences as opportunities to learn about yourself.

This is when the dedication to your spiritual path needs to turn into a strong, steady anchor from which you observe your mental fluctuations. As long as there is ego, the desire to control life and others will remain active, so you have to be disciplined to let go of that impulse. Appreciate any difficulties as gifts helping you discover what you are made of while putting negative patterns to sleep. Stay alert to any self-centered illusions and expectations expressing a hidden, codependent need for validation.

Achieving spiritual freedom takes a long time, because the further you progress, the subtler your resistance becomes. This journey is like a game of "Snakes and Ladders" (a.k.a. "Chutes and Ladders"). At lofty elevations, the longest, most treacherous snakes await, ready to take you down to the bottom, forcing you to start over. This is why many spiritual teachers with a significant degree of awareness have fallen prey to lust, greed, and pride, thus undoing their merit and generating suffering for themselves and others in the process.

Higher up on the Love-Consciousness Pyramid, there is greater dispassion and inner peace. Introspection, discipline, and the study and reflection on the truth are prioritized above group dynamics or the need for validation. All other activities are pursued for their own sake, with no expectations or attachment. As old mental-emotional patterns get weaker, clarity and devotion increase, and a state of *witnessing* emerges. Mindfulness, concentration, and presence are stronger, leading to meditative, blissful, or superconscious states during and beyond a daily meditation practice. In turn, these yield inner silence and peace throughout day-to-day activities as well.

Spiritual powers may develop, which makes it easy to fall into temptation again, believing you have reached the end of your path; you may try to use your knowledge for name and fame, to feel superior. This is where false gurus and self-proclaimed prophets get stuck. A greedy, non-*sattvic* ego will use any level of spiritual development for self-importance to distract you from the ultimate goal. If you are disciplined to master the ego-mind at every opportunity, sensory desires dissipate, clearing the way for the light of Pure Awareness to further remove ego. At this stage, you may seek solitude and silence, as the pain of separation from the Divine intensifies. Your earnest effort and yearning keep driving you upwards, until nothing else matters but the Self or God.

At the top of the Pyramid, which can only be reached through Grace, the Self recognizes the subtle body as a mere illusion, which dissolves the identification with it. All causal seeds and mental imprints of "doership" roast in the light of Pure Awareness, purifying the mind completely and melting the sense of individuality or separation from the Divine. This is the state achieved only by those rare souls who have burnt all desires in the fire of Self-realization, when the eternal Self or God shines as the absolute, all-encompassing reality. That is, these souls abide on this plane as pure Existence-Consciousness-Bliss (or *Sat-Chit-Ananda*).

A fully liberated saint is completely free of ego—of the identification with the body and mind—and therefore unaffected by the natural decline of old age, since the attachment to their body is gone. There is no struggle or suffering because there is no sense of a separate "I"—of *me* and *mine* in relation to *another*. These souls are pure vessels of Divine Consciousness, perceiving only Consciousness in everyone and everything. For this reason, they no longer create karma; although their past karma continues to play out until their physical vehicle dies, it resolves on its own.

The top of the Love-Consciousness Pyramid is the complete annihilation of the individualizing principle that produces the illusion of the world as something external. However, since nothing is real but the Self, the concept of attaining or realizing the Self at the top of the Pyramid only exists at the level of ego consciousness. My analogy is just a tool to help you understand the process so you may give it continuity to break free from your own entrapment. The idea that you are separate from what you have always been is just that, an idea; it vanishes when the ego dissolves in your true, eternal nature, like salt dissolves in water.

Every path leads to Divine Consciousness, because it is the source, the journey, and the ultimate destination of our human experience. All spiritual traditions have the same purpose, although they use different symbols and narratives to explain the meaning of life in the cosmic dreamworld. They belong to one or more of the yoga paths, which often combine, overlap with, or point to one another.

The yoga of devotion (*bhakti yoga*) is the sweetest and easiest in this time and age. That of selfless service (*karma yoga*) burns the ego, if your intentions are truly selfless through the ongoing effort to relinquish the sense of doership and ownership of your actions and their fruits. The yoga of self-discipline (*raja yoga*) offers a variety of tools—such as meditation, mantra, and breathing techniques—to master the ego-mind. Finally, the path of spiritual wisdom or Self-knowledge (*jnana yoga*) provides the most direct access to your divine nature, but it also demands the maturity and discipline acquired through the other yoga paths. It consists in the relentless investigation of the ego-mind.

In truth, you always are at the threshold of your own liberation, since you are essentially free, but you resist and block it by clinging to all sorts of identifications. You reclaim your innate freedom as you overcome life's challenges and unravel the karmic entanglements that shape your reality, to know and dismiss the ego that distorts the truth of who you are. Understanding the shifting quality of your ego and the aspects of the psyche that create your experience through a limited, self-centered view can help you uncover the outdated patterns of perception causing you suffering.

***

Basic Steps to Reduce Negative Karma

Resolving negative karma and avoiding the creation of more starts by accepting your circumstances and painful experiences as divine gifts for growth. Bad karma either resolves through pain and limitations or by dissolving the ego-mind, since it happens at the level of ego consciousness. It diminishes spontaneously when you cultivate detachment, humility, and an attitude of *non-action*—that is, action without the egoic sense of doership or ownership. If you surrender the *doer*, then whose action or whose karma is it?

For this, you have to step out of the victim-blame game that reflects your attachment to suffering. No matter how many obstacles you face or how many times you have been hurt or wronged, holding on to painful memories disconnects you from your true nature; this disconnection is the real root of your pain and negative karma. Embracing life and people as they are, while taking spiritual responsibility for your perception, frees you from the mental distortions that reproduce unpleasant experiences.

Forgiveness is acceptance. You find peace by surrendering to life, dropping your expectations and resentments. An effective way to nurture this is writing a list of the people and grievances you hold any grudges against—not to dwell on them but to recognize your illusions and expectations in each situation, which are not allowing you to accept things as they were. Then go through the list making the conscious decision to let go of the negative emotions you have held toward every person on it, while forgiving yourself for those toxic dynamics as well.

Now, the ego-mind will push the desire to hold accountable those who have wronged you, even if symbolically, and it will perpetuate the belief that forgiving means letting them get away with their harmful actions. But this doesn't affect them or change anything; it only affects you by keeping you enslaved to the past. Forgiveness is not really about others; it is about *you* freeing yourself from what keeps you in a self-perception of vulnerability or deficiency that is contrary to your true Self. If you have suffered violent or intense traumatic events, seek the help of a therapist trained in EMDR (Eye Movement Desensitization and Reprocessing), a classical homeopath, or a specialist in EFT (Emotional Freedom Technique) to clear the psychic imprints of trauma.

Another important aspect here is the anger you identify with. Anger is a defense mechanism of the ego to protect itself. Its fiery energy gives you the illusion of power, but it also disconnects you from love. Anger is pain; it leaves impressions that, if repeated, become negative patterns that will shape future experiences. The tendency toward anger always finds a reason to justify the need to react in anger. When you get angry, you are just giving your power away to the ego-mind that clouds your clarity by fixating on someone to blame. It leads to destructive action, even if only in thought, because it also affects your physical body.

Attachment and fear hide behind anger, since it arises from the self-centeredness of ego. If you can see your attachment and fear, the anger vanishes, but if you identify with it, you lose your discrimination. So, from now on, whenever you get triggered, restrain your impulse toward anger and instead ask yourself, *"What am I so attached to?"* and *"What am I so afraid of?"* Then listen to your inner voice to uncover the real cause of your reactions: your fears and expectations. You can take this further with a truly revolutionary step in your spiritual development: consciously choose not to get angry, no matter what. If you recognize anger as suffering, it is clear that this is an essential step to surrender your ego, which is ultimately your attachment to pain. See your anger as a spiritual poison undermining your efforts to be truly happy and free.

You don't have to suppress your feelings; acknowledge them, but without acting upon, identifying with, or dwelling on them. You are not your emotions; you are the one who can observe them as something external that comes and goes. When you step back to question the internal source of a triggering situation, you go from reactivity to centeredness. Then, through the process of letting go, your experience shifts on its own, because you accept life without the need to control it.

But be warned. Once you make the decision not to get angry, your ego-mind will activate old patterns of perception to justify or instigate an angry reaction with all kinds of obstacles, memories, unpleasant news, pet peeves, and aggressive or difficult people. Try to stay detached and remember the commitment you've made to yourself, choosing freedom over future pain, even if in the moment it may seem challenging. Breathe deeply, mentally step back, and use that fiery energy to fuel your passion for something more beneficial, like a project or a physical activity.

You can even use the same energy to get to the root of your anger and put an end to it by setting clear boundaries or putting an end to power dynamics. You don't have to lash out, you just need to reach an internal point of saturation to say, "Enough of this!" When you surrender to life, you dissolve any desire for revenge with acceptance, clarity, and non-attachment, achieving inner peace as a result. Being the *doer* invariably makes you the *sufferer*, bringing you to low levels of the Love-Consciousness Pyramid and keeping you from the emotional and spiritual freedom for which you yearn.

CHAPTER FOUR

A Spiritual View of Ego

To know what you are, you must first investigate and know what you are not. Discover all that you are not—body, feelings, thoughts, time, space, this or that—nothing, concrete or abstract, which you perceive can be you. The very act of perceiving shows that you are not what you perceive.

— Nisargadatta Maharaj

One of my teachers shared the story of an Indian saint known as Aughar Baba. He belonged to a sect of ascetics who, contrary to most spiritual orders, lived "awkward" (*aughar*) lives with no monastic rules, unconcerned with conventions such as wearing clothes or following a particular diet, lifestyle, and cleanliness standards. He had chosen to live in solitude in the jungle and was perceived as a mad man.

As is customary in that culture, when the people in the closest village understood that he was a spiritual renunciate, they started bringing him food and lighting fires to keep him warm in the winter. He did not pay attention to anyone. At some point, however, the smell of garbage around him started spreading and the villagers wanted him to leave.

One day they saw him dragging the carcass of a dog to his place and starting to roast it. People gathered around him, staring intently, while collecting some of the garbage with sticks. When the ascetic began eating the dog, completely unperturbed, most of the villagers felt sick to their stomachs and ran back home. Only a few stayed, determined to find a way to drive the wild man away.

Suddenly, Aughar Baba stood up and handed a dog leg to a young man who was known to be sincerely devoted to God. Without thinking, the man held his hand out to receive the offering. As the saint walked away, the villagers looked at the fellow's hand and saw that, instead of a dog leg, he was holding raisins and almonds. In that moment, they realized they were graced with the presence of a fully liberated soul with absolute mastery over matter.

Your perception determines your experience of reality. It may change when you stretch into new territory to discover hidden aspects of yourself, when something unexpected challenges your ideas, or when painful events shatter your illusions. Your life is like an imaginary playground for Divine Consciousness to experience itself, but your identification with the physical senses is so strong that you get attached to things and people and end up taking everything too personally and seriously. As a result, it becomes a source of dissatisfaction driven by an ongoing craving for validation, gratification, and distraction.

You master this game of self-awareness by learning from the consequences of your attitudes and actions as you uncover the source of your suffering. You mature spiritually through a slow process of surrendering—to life, to love, to something greater than you—because the ego-mind is relentless at deceiving you into delusion. No matter how much psychological work you do, or how well you think you know yourself, there is always more to uncover, more to heal, more to learn and unlearn as you clear the self-images distorting the real purpose of your existence.

Everything you know and experience happens in your psyche, which is the complex, dynamic, multilayered totality of the mind. It has been depicted as an iceberg floating in the ocean where the tip represents the conscious part while the rest remains submerged or unconscious until it is made available through a preconscious area symbolized by the waves rising to the surface. So, for the most part, who you are is unknown to you, and only a very small percentage of your beliefs, patterns, tendencies, and potential becomes apparent at any given time.

From a spiritual viewpoint, you can only *be* who you are by removing everything you are not, like a sculptor chiseling away at a stone to liberate the figure meant to emerge from it. Learning how the elements of the psyche interact with each other will shed some light onto your inner world and the nature of your reality. Since your main filter is the ego-mind, which you consider your identity, and the ego is elusive by its very nature, seeing it clearly is essential to gain mastery over it.

The term *ego*, which is Latin for "I," became popular after Austrian neurologist Sigmund Freud used it to establish a system of internal analysis based on the idea that the human psyche is dynamic and that each of its aspects develops at different stages. According to him, the ego is the conscience that deals with reality as a function of the conscious, preconscious, and subconscious levels of the psyche. It acts as the mediator between the *id*, or the primal drive for pleasure, and the *superego* that reflects social, moral, and cultural standards.

Although the word has been incorporated into mainstream language as a person's self-importance and arrogance, the

Freudian ego refers to the sensible aspect or reality principle whose function is to satisfy social expectations by restraining the primitive forces of the subconscious. In this sense, it is the organized identity or personality that includes intellectual, cognitive, defensive, and executive faculties to control base impulses through social conditioning.

For Freud, these unconscious impulses are motivated by the desire for instant gratification of the libido and the natural aggression arising from what he coined the "Oedipus complex," or the natural sexual attraction for the parent of the opposite sex, which became the most controversial part of his theory. The id remains infantile, unchanged, and unconscious, so the superego or authority principle pushes the ego to either resolve or repress any unacceptable impulses and feelings.

Many psychotherapeutic models have dismissed Freud's overly sexualized approach. For instance, Alfred Adler didn't view the ego as dominated by the pleasure principle but by the power principle or the "will to power" needed to escape any feelings of insecurity and inferiority. For holocaust survivor Viktor Frankl, the main driving force of the ego is the search for meaning, and for Carl G. Jung, it is the principle of individuation. Jung criticized Freud's view of the libido, seeing it as psychic energy motivating a variety of behaviors, not just sexual gratification. He didn't consider sexual instinct the core of the personality, since the libido could also be used for intellectual, creative, and spiritual pursuits.

According to Jung, the psyche is made up of three systems: the ego, the personal unconscious, and the collective unconscious. Here the ego is the conscious mind that gives you an identity; the personal unconscious is your private collection of memories, including those you have blocked; and the collective or transpersonal unconscious stems from ancestral memories and archetypes expressed as predispositions. Jung didn't think of the subconscious as a mere repository of repressed desires and emotions, but rather as the dynamic link between the individual and the collective past. For him, humans were born with a behavioral repertoire adapted to their environment, like other animal species.

He focused on four main archetypes to describe the psyche: the *persona*, which is the mask you present to the world to conceal who you are for reasons of adaptation or convenience; the *anima* or *animus* represents the feminine qualities in a male and the masculine qualities in a female that balance the personality; the *shadow* expresses the aspects you dislike in yourself that you tend to project onto other people; and the *self* provides a sense of unity in your experiences as well as the drive toward the fulfillment of your potential.

The Jungian self is the unified conscious and unconscious psyche motivating the process of individuation while integrating the various elements of the personality. It differs from Freud's view of this process being directed by the ego, which for Jung is a smaller part arising from the self. The Jungian ego is a "complex" experiencing itself at the center of the psyche; that is, a core unconscious pattern of perceptions, emotions, memories, and desires organized around a common theme, such as status, power, or trauma. He often represented the self as a circle with a dot in its center symbolizing the ego.

Jung and other integrative and humanistic schools consider the transcendental aspects of spirituality essential for mental health, although they cannot provide such type of experience.

When psychologists speak of a strong or healthy ego, they usually refer to a well-adjusted individual who is able to achieve certain social goals within the moral guidelines of their culture. However, this adjustment often requires defense mechanisms to suppress tension, anxiety, guilt, or a sense of inferiority, which can lead to mental issues when there is too much friction between any of the aspects of the psyche. Since these processes remain unconscious, most people simply skirt around their pain and past unresolved feelings with distractions and compulsive or addictive behaviors.

I consider the many years I spent in psychoanalysis an important turning point that sparked my spiritual journey, but I also appreciate the disregard of psychology *per se* of most Eastern spiritual systems, given that they recognize the ego-mind as the main obstacle to uncovering our divine essence. A strong ego is necessary to engage and succeed in the world, because the world itself is a creation of the ego-mind. But the aim of spirituality is to dissolve this false I-sense to reach the permanent bliss of the Supreme Self, which the ego disturbs with all forms of attachment and fear. It is the mental or psychological stuff that gets in the way of the steady happiness for which we all yearn.

For example, the goal of self-actualization is the fulfillment of the creative, intellectual, and social potential of the individual. Although a worthy endeavor, it presumes a personality or identity as a composite of many sub-personalities or *personae* to enable a person to play different roles in a variety of scenarios in order to satisfy their needs and desires. Since spirituality strives for transcendence—lasting freedom from suffering—these aspects are viewed as false identifications hindering spiritual enlightenment, which is the ultimate purpose of life.

A Spiritual View of Ego

Assuming different roles at different times may be a sign of mental flexibility, but the fixation on these roles as identities strengthens the false I-sense that isolates you by dividing and categorizing your experience of life. It colors your perception with the attachment to the roles you play and the value you think they give you ("I am a parent," "I am a teacher," "I am a CEO"). Similarly, it fixates your negative tendencies and behaviors with labels that become identifications ("I am an addict," "I am depressed," "I am anxious," "I am not good enough").

Anything with which you qualify your *I-am-ness*—that is, anything you place after "I am"—becomes part of your self-perception and shapes how you experience yourself in different situations. Over time, your reality revolves around these temporary identities, enslaving you to certain roles, labels, past traumas, or self-images, which are just repeated thoughts about yourself. The issue here is not assuming the various roles needed to experience different aspects of life; it is the attachment or identification that prevents you from realizing that these labels do not define you, because they are not the real you. The real you is the one who can observe, question, and dismiss them as mere ideas, but only if you can see them for what they are.

A psychological exploration may be necessary before embarking on a spiritual journey, especially if there is much trauma or mental health issues. However, as a spiritual seeker, it is important to understand that what it helps you uncover is *everything you are not but you've believed yourself to be*: the wounds, fixations, ideas, and emotions that trap you in the past. A mental understanding may clear the way, but self-knowledge does not happen at the level of the intellect; it arises in Pure Awareness, beyond the mental realms, although the mind will swiftly give it names and concepts. Anyone can try to be a functional, well-adjusted person in a dysfunctional world, but if you want spiritual freedom, then your path is about recognizing the limitations of your ego consciousness driving you to look for happiness in a world of impermanent appearances.

Let me give you an analogy. Imagine you are in a room and you notice there is water rising above the ground. You cannot see where the water is coming from, so you set out to discover its source before it gets too high. You start searching, observing, and analyzing clues and signs as you explore the room. Suddenly, you spot an open faucet attached to one of the walls. You rush to shut it off, relieved that you have found what is causing the flood. But soon after, you realize that the water is still rising. This is how the psychological process tends to go.

You navigate life as best you can until a painful situation nudges you to look for the source of your sorrow. You may spend years rehashing your story, processing difficult events, and gaining insight into yourself and the people you believe to have caused a distorted self-perception. You gradually become more self-aware and think you are resolving the issues that have created difficulties in your life. You are certainly more stable and mature to function in the world. But if an unexpected event occurs, old emotions suddenly take over and drag you down a rabbit hole of confusion, insecurity, or self-pity. You feel vulnerable and unable to control your emotions, even if you have learned tools to cope with your distress.

You are a complex, multilayered spark of Consciousness, and your life plays out according to the seeds of perception from past impressions and karma hidden in your causal body. The issues you are here to address will come back time and time again, especially during stressful situations, because they reflect deeply ingrained, predominant *tendencies* of thought, perception, and action. You may have rationalized or put some to sleep for a while, but you cannot control what may arouse negative causal seeds again. You must consciously starve them of energy by recognizing them as they sprout in your reality.

Any system of knowledge works best within its own conceptual framework, even if it overlaps with other systems. I briefly shared some of the psychological notions of psyche and ego to provide points of reference and contrast with a spiritual approach that includes but also goes beyond the realm of the mind or the psychological understanding of yourself. The ultimate purpose of human life is, in fact, to transcend the mind, since the concepts of time, space, past, present, and future, as well as the sense of individuality and the experience of duality, happen only in the mind, where all afflictions take place as well.

This broader philosophical view reveals that suffering isn't just rooted in childhood events; it arises from the very nature of your ego that distorts your perception. In spiritual terms, the ego is a false identity that disconnects you from the eternal Self you truly are. It lets you experience the world, but anything that has to do with it is bound to cause pain because it is temporary; it has a beginning and an end. The world itself is made of ego, invariably fostering and reinforcing ego. Believing yourself to be this false I-sense prevents you from moving up the Love-Consciousness Pyramid toward real freedom and love. Now, how does the ego arise and why is it so hard to pinpoint and remove?

From the desire to experience itself in all forms and shapes, Divine Consciousness manifests the universe through its creative feminine principle, or Primordial Matter. The first expression of this desire is the thought "I am." In this sense, "I am" is the initial modification of the eternal Self launching Creation as a dream of multiplicity through the *gunas*. The ignorance of the Self, as well as all thoughts, imaginations, emotions, impressions, intuitions, and knowledge appearing in the mind, are variations of this "I" consciousness or *I-am-ness*, through which Pure Awareness becomes aware of itself. In other words, the cosmic thought "I am" becomes the ego consciousness that reflects it while also blocking it by creating the illusion of separation.

"I am" is the essential certainty of your existence. Anything you attach to it belongs to the ego and is illusory and temporary. In Sanskrit, ego is known as *ahamkara* to convey the idea that this "I am" (*aham*) is not the original, pure *I-am-ness* but "a created thing" (*kara*). To put it simply, the ego is just a projection of the eternal Self pretending to be the Self. It is like looking at yourself in a mirror believing that your reflection is the real you. As the ego attaches the mind to sensory perception, it requires a subject and object, or a sense of self and *other* to objectify its reality. Through this delusion of duality, the ego becomes the subtle link between the body and mind with which you identify that keeps you trapped in the cosmic dream.

The people and objects in your life take shape through the elements and qualities of nature; they appear solid and three-dimensional due to variations of light, just like a painting or a photograph. If you were in a dark room, you would perceive the objects in the room by shedding light upon them. Consciousness gives reality to the world in a similar manner; when its light counters the dark density of matter, you become aware of the objects with which you come into contact through the physical senses. As they leave mental impressions, the recognition of similar objects occurs by inference or association.

Owing to the paradoxical nature of Consciousness, your mind is both a field of experience and a filter limiting your perception of reality. Your ego is both a projection of the Self and a mirage that obstructs it. The ego is homeless, so it can make a temporary home anywhere in the psyche; it also has access to all your mental files. In the lower mind, it is the receiver of the objective, external reality, as well as the instinctual impulses and desires triggered by sensory perception. In the higher mind, it is the subjective aspect of your experience, or the *experiencer* of *your* reality. Its mobile quality allows it to hide in plain sight while activating your predominant tendencies. To see it clearly, you must uncover your patterns of perception and behavior.

Suppose you want to take a photograph of something, but your camera lens is out of focus. What distorts the picture is not your camera nor the lens. It is not your eyesight nor the object you are trying to photograph; it is the blurriness that affects all of them in some way. In this case, adjusting the focus to get a sharper image is an easy solution, but you first need to become aware that this is what causes the distortion. In life, however, the ego uses all kinds of tricks to skew your perception, fixating your attention outward to make you believe that what causes you difficulties or pain is outside of you. It blocks the truth that this false identity, to which you cling so tightly, is the real source of your discontentment.

Since the ego hijacks the Self, the mind as a whole ends up serving the ego. You need to develop self-awareness and discrimination to conquer it, turning the mind inward to detach from a distorted self-perception. The ego-mind lacks the discerning quality that grants you the capacity to question, process, and redirect your attention toward Pure Awareness. Any cognitive process is, well, a *process* you can observe, learn from, or interpret in a variety of ways to meet the needs of your ego, but awareness occurs instantaneously and emerges beyond the mind.

My illustration of the yogic view of the psyche displays the various elements that shape your experience. Visualize them as fluid layers of energy in constant interaction, like waves in the ocean overlapping at different levels of awareness. The main aspects in your mental field (*chitta*) are: the intellect or higher mind (*buddhi*), which is the main screen where Consciousness projects itself for the world to appear; the psycho-emotional or lower mind (*manas*) that registers the world through the senses; and the ego (*ahamkara*), which is the individual identity that col-

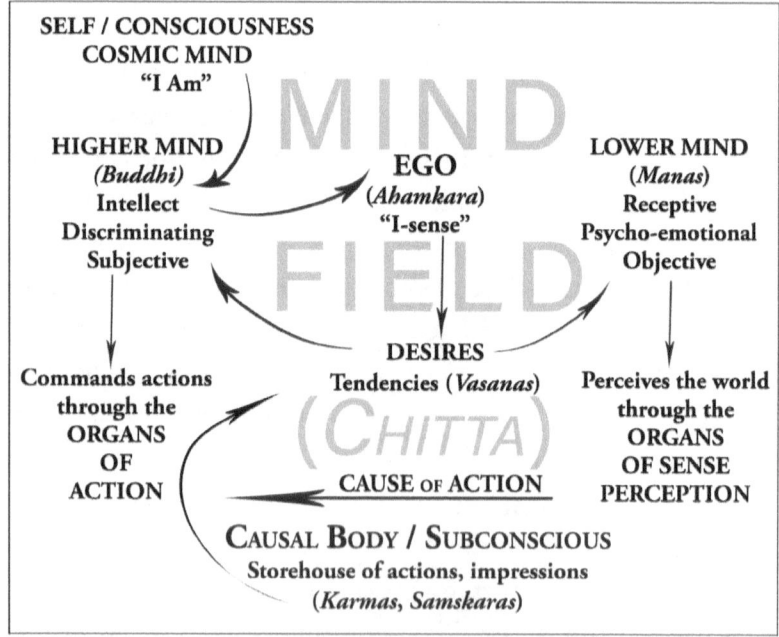

The Field of Experience (Mind, Psyche)

ors your perception with desires and beliefs from past impressions and predominant tendencies in the causal body.

Because of your identification with your body and mind, the ego directs your behavior through its inherent ignorance and egoism. Spiritual egoism is the erroneous notion that the individualized mind is the eternal Self, when in reality the mind is unconscious. It is a window into the innumerable shapes and forms the light of Consciousness brings forth, but it is not the light itself. No matter how clean a window may be, it can never be as clear as the direct observation of reality, so even the purified mind of a yogi is not as pure as the Self. Believing the ego-mind to be the Self is like believing that a sunbeam is the sun rather than a temporary projection of it.

Spiritual ignorance refers to the idea that matter is conscious; that consciousness is an inherent quality of the mind and body because sentient beings are aware of their sensations. But your mental states change according to your predominant tendencies of perception, of which you are not conscious until you start looking within. Without self-knowledge, you simply react to life following hidden impulses. You think your mind and body have consciousness, but in reality, Divine Consciousness acts as different bodies and minds; these are the vehicles through which the eternal Self experiences itself. Similar to a solar panel that transforms sunlight into energy as a result of the sun being projected onto the panel, and not because the panel holds the sun inside, your individual consciousness is a reflection of Pure Awareness on your mind.

Owing to its spiritual ignorance and egoism, the ego believes to be the eternal Self, but only Consciousness is conscious and real. As your essence, it grants you the power to cognize the world as well as to redirect your attention away from the ego. However, your identification with the body and mind distorts your perception with the delusion of duality or *otherness* that blocks this truth and causes suffering. The ego traps and isolates you in the dichotomy of a subjective-objective reality with feelings of attraction and aversion, as well as judgments and comparisons toward different people and objects, all the while seeking pleasure and trying to avoid pain.

The human condition holds this ingrained restlessness that keeps the ego in charge. The ego produces a sense of deficiency by obstructing the divine totality you are; then it drives you to seek sensory gratification to counter the dissatisfaction it creates. Your identification with the physical body also generates the fear of death, which is the source of all other fears. By trying to protect itself from its limitations, the ego promotes the fantasy that pursuing pleasure and avoiding pain is how you will defeat, or at least defer, your own mortality.

The desire for pleasure creates attraction to things and people, which easily becomes attachment; and the desire to avoid pain produces aversion, which is an inverse form of attachment that turns into fear or resistance. Most people live life motivated by attraction, aversion, and fear, chasing desires and expecting other people to do what they want to make them happy. But true happiness can only be found by breaking free from the ego-mind, because the impermanent experiences to which it clings disconnect you from your limitless essence. Happiness is your true nature, so how happy you are will depend on the purity of your perception—your degree of freedom from spiritual egoism and ignorance.

A Spiritual View of Ego

Because of its shape-shifting and mobile qualities, the ego can be viewed as the attachment to sensory perception that craves instant gratification, like the Freudian pleasure principle, as well as the conscience that restrains it in an attempt to gain a sense of control, in accordance with Adler's power principle. Furthermore, being itself the principle of individuality, it holds the Jungian drive for individuation through self-centered experiences that maintain the illusion of separation, as well as Frankl's search for meaning when it is confronted with its own limitations. In spiritual or yogic terms, the ego is *the principle of individuality hijacking the Self to maintain the delusion of duality through your identification with the body and mind.*

It is inherently restless and unfulfilled, jumping from one mental aspect to another and one desire to another. A desire is the combination of egoic ignorance with the energy of activity (*rajas*); it produces tension and dissatisfaction propelling you toward it. When the dense quality (*tamas*) is prevalent, the focus is on material pleasure and comfort, often resulting in greed, lust, sloth, gluttony, or addiction. If the active quality predominates, it seeks the pleasure experienced through passion, achievement, prestige, or external power. When a desire is satisfied, the tension it created diminishes momentarily until another desire appears, but if it is jeopardized in any way, the ego refuses to accept this, obscuring reality with emotions like anger to protect itself.

Since your ego arises with the consciousness of sensory perception, anything you identify with becomes part of your identity. Thoughts such as, "I am attractive, successful, smart, spiritual," or "I am ugly, poor, a failure, a victim" are self-images through which the ego makes itself felt. But none of them are fixed or the real you; they are mental states that change according to external situations. In this sense, ego is not just the arrogance or pride usually associated with the term; it can attach to anything to prevent you from seeing yourself clearly and being fully present. You allow these mental fluctuations to define you—mostly in relation to *others*—by identifying with your emotions, which may invade your perception to the point of losing yourself.

Taking their shape, the ego-mind fixates on something that is naturally bound to pass. In that moment of entrapment, however, it seems that there is nothing more real than how you feel, and you think it will last forever! The intellect has the capacity to discern these false identities, but it is often clouded by the great number of thoughts, desires, and fears with which the ego-mind bombards you. You may know intellectually when something is not good for you, yet you get pulled in the direction of negative habits if these tendencies hold more energy than positive ones. Clearly, the more you follow them, the stronger they become.

Think of your psyche as the factory where your experiences are produced. The ego is the supervisor managing the lower, psycho-emotional mind through your physical senses as well as your organs of perception and action. Without clear instruction from the higher, discriminating mind that is supposed to be in charge of the factory, the supervisor simply follows the loudest voice—that is, the most predominant desires and patterns in your subconscious. This is how the ego-mind overpowers the intellect to carry out thoughts, words, and actions from negative tendencies, which is the direction the ego naturally follows to obstruct the light of the Self.

A Spiritual View of Ego

These tendencies get stronger as the cycle continues and more information is received through the senses, so you end up investing energy in things that cause you confusion or suffering without understanding why, even if those impulses go against conscious desires or logical reasoning. You need self-awareness and discipline to restrain the impulses of the ego-mind and stop following it blindly in search of sensory gratification.

Desires fuel life and keep you moving forward, but since the very nature of desire is dissatisfaction, it preserves the false idea that you are separate from what you want, which is happiness. You think you will achieve it by fulfilling desires, but the joy or pleasure they provide is impermanent. They appear to be natural, but they are mind-made, and you keep chasing them to cover up the internal restlessness of your ego. You have spent lifetimes pursuing desires from one birth to the next, in a mental loop that traps you in suffering. If you want liberation from your mental entrapment, it is essential to comprehend that chasing anything outside of you cannot bring lasting joy.

Suffering comes from the mirage of separation the ego creates that has you wavering between pleasure and pain, excitement and distress, hope and despair. To break free, you must view yourself and act like an actor in the play of Consciousness rather than a doer. You don't have to be indifferent or renounce your dreams, but instead of chasing promises of fleeting enjoyment, question your desires and examine what is it in you that makes you unhappy. Your investigation will gradually dissolve the ego, the root of your discontentment. Anchoring yourself in the present moment, observe your thoughts and impulses while removing your attachments and expectations. This will give way to *non-action*, or spontaneous, ego-less action, as a pure vessel of divine energy.

None of the mental activity with which you identify is the real you. It cannot be you if it comes and goes. You are the one who observes it appear and disappear in your mental field. If you truly comprehend this, without letting the ego-mind push or pull you in any direction, you will find the happiness for which you yearn. You can never be completely passive in life, but you can play this divine game by doing what you are compelled to do without getting attached to your roles or the outcomes of your endeavors. You may share your ideas, talents, and gifts in a spirit of service while renouncing the illusion of being the doer or the owner of your experiences and the fruits of your actions.

Clearly, this is a process that requires discipline, because the ego-mind will disguise itself in a variety of ways. In my analogy of the factory, the manager and associates are reluctant to give back the control they have acquired, and they are willing to sabotage the functioning of the factory to keep their power. This is your resistance to "let go and let God," as they say, by surrendering to life as it is. But once you understand how the ego-mind operates, it becomes predictable, which gives you an advantage over its deceiving, shape-shifting, mobile nature.

What distinguishes humans from other animals is the capacity for cognitive thought. This thinking principle allows you to perceive and experience the world, but the constant production of thoughts that comes with it keeps you in ignorance of your true nature as well. In yoga philosophy, this aspect is known as *vritti*, which is the whirlpool-like or revolving quality of the mind that forms all thought waves, thus disturbing the stillness of Pure Awareness. As they go round and round, your thoughts, emotions, memories, beliefs, imaginations, and intuitions weave the patterns through which you experience your life.

Parallel to nature, where a seed blossoms to generate new seeds, this principle produces an ongoing chain of thoughts conditioned by impressions or causal seeds from previous thoughts. Every thought is a modification of a previous thought with the potential to yield similar thoughts that will also condition future cognitive processes. In this sense, there is a feedback loop that continuously colors your reality with past energy, thus distorting the experience of new situations.

In truth, the mind is just a collection of memories and thoughts. As it spins, it keeps you busy with old patterns that feed on and reinforce each other while tainting your reality. It is like being in a hamster wheel, pedaling away as you try to move forward, yet trapped in past, painful emotions from false yet unconscious beliefs. You step out of your own wheel by exploring the ego-mind as you observe these patterns repeat in your life. If you redirect your attention and energy inward, you are able to recognize negative tendencies and outdated ideas about yourself. It is crucial to remember that your mental patterns will come back around and around, each time giving you an opportunity to make conscious what has been hidden from you.

Painful or negative thoughts originate in selfish motivations, while those that are neutral or not painful bring greater clarity and peace. You cultivate these by observing the ups and downs of life from a centered state of non-attachment, restraining the ego-mind without carrying out unconscious impulses. Because of the revolving nature of the mind, painful thoughts produce and reinforce seeds of ignorance and egoism, while non-painful thoughts leave peaceful imprints leading to greater emotional and spiritual freedom.

Thoughts fuel actions, and actions tend to repeat as well; they are investments of energy revolving through your reality as a result of predominant habits of perception and behavior. Deeper impressions revolve throughout many cycles along your soul journey, over several lifetimes, as you undergo the full spectrum of human experience. However, this repetitiveness eventually turns too distressing and unfulfilling, pushing you to find a way out of suffering.

Your reality is shaped with karmic dynamics and situations, so rather than fighting it or trying to force anything, which causes you more suffering, you can transform your perception, which is where your sense of experience originates. If you embrace life as a journey of self-discovery, rather than the pursuit of fleeting desires or as something you are supposed to fix or control, you nurture the light, positive qualities of your true nature. Only by heeding a deeper yearning for the reality of the Self will you break free from the control of the ego.

Spiritual freedom requires dropping this false identity by developing dispassion for the external world, which is a projection of your ego. Now, cultivating detachment is not easy, for you are used to navigating life with the ego consciousness that glues you to people and things. Even the word *detachment* may trigger resistance, due to the misconception that love is attachment and therefore detachment equals indifference or lack of love. The emotional attachment between a mother and a child is essential for that child to develop a strong sense of self, but it becomes a hindrance to spiritual growth later in life. Detachment means removing the concepts of *me* and *mine* that distort love to free yourself from the fluctuations of the ego-mind.

In the world of appearances, attachment and lust are mistaken for love. And yet, love is your true nature, while attachment creates fear, anger, possessiveness, and greed, which are opposite to love. In this sense, love with no attachment is the purest form of love; it is the neutral, universal essence of the Self untainted by ego. Being detached doesn't mean that you become an insensitive person who doesn't care about anyone else; it means that you dissolve your identification with the ego to remain centered rather than impulsively letting your desires and emotions dictate your behavior.

A good example is that of a bank manager. She works every day with the money in the bank, doing her job as best as she can, without being attached to the money that is not hers. Her actions don't show any non-attachment, but she has no *internal* sense of ownership or entitlement. She is clear about her role at the bank and does not covet the money, so she does not need to restrain the impulse to steal it. Her main focus is on her performance as a manager, so the idea of that money belonging to her just isn't there. If it were, it might lead her to destructive actions.

Similarly, when you mentally step back to observe and accept things and people as they are, and as they come and go, you remove any self-centered, distorted ideas of how life *should* be. If you don't feed any illusions or expectations, you prevent negative actions and disappointments. By embracing life as it is, with all its changes, ups, and downs, you avoid the suffering that follows the identification with the ego-mind. The sense of ownership disturbs your inner peace and disconnects you from yourself until you are able to recognize that it is a mere idea, and not an absolute truth.

You can remain detached as you engage with people by bringing your attention to your heart, breathing into it, and making the conscious decision to not be reactive but aware of your feelings without becoming your feelings. Any impulsive, knee-jerk reaction comes from ego; it shows that you are focused on others in a self-centered manner—on what they do or say in relation to *your* desires and expectations. You identify with their behavior because you secretly expect some kind of validation or gratification. To master the ego-mind, you must bring to light any hidden motivations and remove any self-interest.

When you look at a situation from a more neutral or centered place, rather than taking it personally by identifying with it, the mind naturally recedes, creating an opening for Consciousness to flow, which spontaneously shifts your reality. Self-awareness is key here, because there is a delay between the input from the ego-mind and the discernment of the higher mind—that is, between your reaction and your reflection upon it. You may think of all the things you *could* or *should* have done or said differently after the fact. But instead of fixating on regrets or negative emotions, you can think of new ways to respond next time a similar situation comes along. Since the mind is made of revolving patterns, you can be sure it will repeat in some way until you are able to recognize and stop investing in the beliefs that create it.

Pay close attention to your thoughts, feelings, and impulses, being completely honest with yourself. Accept them without rationalizing or identifying with them, ready to step back emotionally from any experience to see it clearly. Transcending the ego-mind demands taking full spiritual responsibility for everything in your reality, which starts by seeing it as an individualized mental projection colored with outdated impressions and unconscious patterns distorting your experience of the present with the emotional energy of the past.

* * *

The Best Version of You

This exercise will help you clarify the aspects you need to nurture in yourself to remain centered as you make choices in life. You may fine-tune or add to it as time goes by and you keep growing. To be effective, however, it must be solely about you, not based on other people, relationships, or situations you would like to improve. It is not a to-do list or a set of resolutions and goals; it is a guideline to help you remember how you would like to respond in any type of scenario to feel good about yourself, connected to the flow of your life.

Write a list or a few paragraphs describing the features, qualities, or traits of the person you want to become—the ideal you. Concentrate on those aspects that would make you feel more authentic and freer, regardless of what others may think or do. Include what you already value in yourself as well as the qualities you admire in others that you would like to develop. The idea is to imagine the possibilities of living from a place of greater truth rather than the familiar roles, comparisons, and self-images that create pressure, guilt, or a sense of obligation. Forget about what you think is expected of you, and concentrate on the qualities and values that ring true to you *now*.

For instance, "Being more relaxed, independent, tolerant, flexible, patient, detached, compassionate, disciplined, confident, open-minded, creative, expressive, spontaneous, joyful," and so on. Think of any attributes and qualities you want to cultivate to be one-with-yourself. Through your reflection, an ideal, more mature archetype will emerge, which you can emulate to stay centered and on track with both worldly and spiritual goals.

Once you are clear about this ideal version of you, use it as a reference when dealing with challenging situations or before making decisions. Ask yourself, "Does this choice get me closer to the Best Version of Me, or am I simply following a familiar pattern, role, or illusion like many times before?" "How do I want to respond in this particular moment to be more independent, relaxed, tolerant, flexible, detached (and so on)?" If a certain action gets you closer to who you want to become, go for it; if not, mentally step back to change course and find greater alignment with the person you want to be. This generally means letting go of something pulling you in a direction that goes against your truth or the experience you desire (balanced interactions, loving relationships, good communication, a strong sense of purpose, more enjoyment, etc.). Only you know how you really feel, so listen to your inner voice and be completely honest!

It is important to remember that nobody else is in charge of the Best Version of You. Don't expect others to do things differently to make it easier, either; this is about you making conscious changes in the moment. For example, during an argument, your ego-mind will want to spin in a wounded, angry place that is familiar, but you can question this position to shift the focus toward a solution or a better way to address whatever the issue may be. Using the Best Version of You as a guideline helps you redirect your attention inward, making room for better interactions and new possibilities of experience.

Rather than following the usual impulses to defend yourself, prove something, impose your viewpoint, or attack the other person, you can detach from the situation and keep centered by questioning your reactions. Whenever you get triggered, inquire, "What am I so attached to or afraid of?" If you are completely honest with yourself, you will recognize the ideas that keep you in outdated patterns of perception, tainting your current experience; once you do, negative emotions will vanish. If they don't, it is because you haven't yet seen the beliefs feedings them; dig more deeply. Then, as you mentally step back, ask yourself, "Is this the only way I can experience this moment?" and "How can I nurture the Best Version of Me, right here, right now?"

The issue is not about being right or wrong; the problem is whether you let the ego-mind direct your behavior instead of choosing the type of interactions you really want, from a place of openness and love. What is more important: to be right or to create a more pleasant reality for yourself, where you can be at peace? Because of its dividing, self-centered nature, the ego leads to negative, destructive emotions and actions with the expectation of gratification or validation. When you stop making things about "me, me, me," the ego-mind has no choice but to recede and quit blocking the light and love you and others are.

Cultivating the Best Version of You will let you experience relationships from a deeper level and a stronger sense of self. Also, learn to pick your battles wisely. Your greatest struggle is and will always be the one with your elusive ego-mind distorting your perception of reality and producing pain. Inner peace arises when you uncover your hidden motivations and develop dispassion to step out of the mental loops of *me* and *mine*, or "me against another" that keep the ego in control. This will become clearer as you understand your *sense of otherness*, which is the aspect of ego that keeps the illusion of separation from the Self in all its manifestations

THE PROCESS: INDIVIDUATION IN DUALITY

CHAPTER FIVE

Your Egoic Sense of Otherness

The ego is our own creation. This is what we have to remove. Once this falls away, our inner light will shine forth. When dark clouds fill the sky, we cannot experience the sunlight. If we sit in a house and close the doors and windows, we cannot see the sunlight either.

— *Mata Amritanandamayi*

Every evening, an old couple sits in their living room in front of a picture window looking into the street. They enjoy chatting and commenting on the people passing by. A new family has recently moved to the house across from theirs, and a young woman is hanging freshly laundered clothes in her yard. The wife watches the neighbor for a moment and then exclaims, "Those clothes are dirty! That woman doesn't know how to do laundry. What a disgrace!"

Now every time the wife sees her neighbor hanging clothes, she comments on the woman's washing abilities. She complains, "What a shame! Can't she see how unclean those garments are? Someone needs to teach her how to do the wash!" The husband usually remains quiet.

One evening, as the wife joins him on the couch, she looks out the window and notices something is different. The clothes hanging on the line are spotless. She does not know what to say at first, but after a few minutes she acknowledges, "It was about time! Someone must have shown this woman how to do the laundry. Either that, or they did it for her." To which the husband responds with a grin, "I just cleaned the window!"

The ego-mind is your window onto the world. It is both the screen and the filter through which you perceive and judge everything around you. Its morphing quality makes it elusive, as it constantly trades one mental construct for another. Some people see the ego as an enemy you have to kill, because it is your selfishness and arrogance. Others think it is a psychic mechanism protecting you from what you couldn't understand or cope with while growing up. And then there is the psychological notion that the ego is the consciousness and conscience that shapes your identity.

Now, if you believe it is your identity, you are not going to want to dissolve it. If you think it protects you in some way, you are also going to hold on to it. And if you think you can just kill it, you would be fooling yourself, because that would be like giving the role of detective to a thief. Who would be watching whom? It is not a matter of semantics; the problem is that you would be chasing shadows, trying to pin down something that isn't fixed. Thinking that you are the one destroying it keeps the illusion of you being the *doer*, which is one of your most fundamental identifications with the ego.

From a spiritual perspective, the ego is a projection of the eternal Self that maintains the mirage of a multiplicity of forms by fragmenting its totality. It is a mobile, individualizing principle that hides in your mental field by objectifying your existence as something external, including your body, people, objects, and situations. It produces the material world, and you believe that you are this false identity acting in the world. But you have the capacity to observe its fluctuations and look within to access deeper aspects of your soul, which proves that the ego is neither fixed nor the real you. Your ongoing challenge is dismissing the distractions it creates to keep you from going inward.

You may be wondering, how I can say that the ego isn't real, if this book explores what it is and how it operates? Well, this is the paradoxical nature of Consciousness at play. All phenomena are just appearances of the One eternal Self fashioned with the qualities of nature, individualized by the ego, and labeled by the mind, like different pieces of jewelry made of the same gold. The gold is not affected by its modifications; it can be melted again and again to create different shapes and designs without ever losing its essence.

As the root cause of suffering, the ego takes many forms. The most obvious is that of attachment, as well as negative thoughts and desires leading to anger, arrogance, and greed. However, its shape-shifting quality allows it to become subtler and subtler as self-awareness increases. Gross forms of pain, such as physical sensations or intense emotions, are easier to appreciate than subtler expressions, because these blend with your tendencies of perception. Here is a common example.

Suppose you lost your job and are struggling to find a new one. This is clearly painful; it produces anxiety about meeting your basic needs. When you are able to get another job, your anxiety subsides, but then you may complain that the job is stressful or boring, or you may have issues with people in the workplace. It becomes a source of discontentment. If you stick with the job, to avoid the anxiety you previously experienced, then you may be afraid of spending your money or not having enough for the future. Now you are dissatisfied because you wish you had more. Or you may be afraid of losing your job again or of someone stealing your stuff. At each step, the pain gets subtler. Anxiety turns into lack of joy, fear of losing something you are attached to, or distress from an imaginary sense of deficiency.

Something similar can happen with relationships. You long for love and companionship, but when you finally connect with someone, you are afraid to commit emotionally because of past hurts and disappointments. If there is conflict, you feel resistance toward your partner or crave something else—for instance, the freedom of being single or the idea of a better mate. If you stay in the relationship, your ego-mind will find innumerable reasons to complain, sabotage, and have doubts about it. Being alone was painful, but now you are attached to the other person or to certain aspects of the relationship, and you fear losing them. In any case, the ego-mind makes itself felt by creating discontentment at every step to disconnect you from the present.

The desire for pleasure creates attraction, and the fear of pain produces aversion; you waver between them, resisting life *as it is* with illusions of what you think it *should* be. But your life is never separate from you, so the nature of your experiences is really a matter of how open or closed off you are to life. The ego-mind controls your perception by drawing your attention outward; if you turn it inward to gain self-awareness, you are able to discern subtler and subtler forms of pain as you get to know yourself. Before you perceive deeper aspects, you feel tangible forms of suffering, such as anxiety, jealousy, or anger pulling you to the lower levels of the Love-Consciousness Pyramid. You can focus on something more creative or enjoyable, but the only way to eliminate all distress is by refusing to identify with the ego that isolates you.

A less obvious form of pain is the continuous mental chatter robbing you of your inner peace. It may not feel like pain because you are so used to your thoughts always telling you what is going on. But unless you are concentrated on something specific, this uninvited mental activity tends to go in a negative direction, bringing fear, insecurity, or guilt to disconnect you from yourself. Without self-reflection, you will continue to believe that your emotions are caused by something external, since the ego-mind blurs your clarity with an ongoing flow of thoughts and desires.

The painful quality of this activity becomes apparent only after you have experienced inner silence, usually through deep meditation, in the presence of an enlightened master, or in nature, because it provides a clear contrast with the usual mental noise. The mind needs concepts and labels to exist, but Pure Awareness precedes all thought; it is silent and still. For this reason, growing spiritually means gaining self-knowledge by being aware of the mental-emotional fluctuations that disturb your inner peace. You need to observe your thoughts to counter the constant restlessness that sets you off-center, embracing all situations as they unfold, without rejecting the unpleasant ones or holding on to the pleasurable ones.

Otherwise, your ego will continue to control your choices, pushing you to seek external gratification and validation. In this context, the ego is not merely a mediator between instinctual impulses and the demands of the external world, although these are important elements of your behavior. It is not a real identity but a false I-sense that your true Self temporarily assumes to experience itself. The idea of having an identity or personality arises from your identification with the past, which taints the present and is also projected into the future. If you live anchored in the moment, those identifications disappear.

In my story of the old couple, the ego makes the wife believe that what appears dirty is outside the window. In your life, the ego creates the delusion that both your negative, painful aspects and the things you yearn for are outside of you as well. It not only impairs your view through the window of your mind; it also triggers the resistance to clear it and appreciate people and situations as they really are. Because it is your self-centeredness, it distorts your view while hiding in plain sight, mainly by directing you to focus on *others*.

It may show as entitlement, when you expect other people to make you happy by doing what you want; as righteousness, when you believe you are right and others are wrong; as arrogance, when you feel superior or better than everyone else; as victimhood, when you give your power away to avoid taking responsibility for yourself; or as unworthiness, when you diminish yourself in comparison to others or don't get the validation you were secretly hoping for.

This hidden, emotional codependency creates all sorts of dramas binding you to the polarizing aspects of the world. Your soul reincarnates in karmic resonance with those souls and desires with which you must find some resolution. You cannot break free from the wheel of suffering or deaths and rebirths (*Samsara*) until you dissolve the ego that creates this plane of experience; and you cannot transcend the ego without being at peace with yourself and others on this plane of experience. The separation is just an illusion, so removing it from your perception is the way out of it.

Your Egoic Sense of Otherness

Like every stage in your life, each human embodiment is a new chapter in a complex, multifaceted psycho-emotional story played out according to the impressions of previous chapters, as well as your purpose within the dream of Consciousness. In perfect divine synchronicity, your soul takes on a new body in the environment most likely to reactivate its predominant causal seeds to continue exploring the full spectrum of your human adventure. As the ego arises, the mind identifies with sensory perception through attraction, aversion, and fear. In concert with the other aspects of the psyche, the ego brings forth imprints stored in the subconscious to actualize your tendencies. When, where, and how you are conceived and reborn is the result of unfulfilled desires and karma from previous experiences—prior manifestations of ego. Every time your soul reincarnates, your ego consciousness awakens, just like when you wake up every morning after sleeping all night.

Since you don't naturally remember your past lives, things seem random; and ultimately, they are, because it is all a dream of Consciousness. At the level of appearances, there is no logical reason as to why some lives are long and others short; why some are hard and others easier; or why some are focused on worldly achievements while others may be simpler or more introspective. But what matters is that each lifetime, as well as every moment, offers you a new opportunity to heal your disconnection from Consciousness, even if you also run the risk of getting more karmically enmeshed in the world of suffering.

After many repetitive cycles, it starts losing its appeal. Every birth entails enduring physical and mental pain, so you eventually reach a point of saturation compelling you to look for a way out. A similar process occurs within each lifetime and each stage of spiritual maturity. The result is a growing yearning for freedom, prompting you to escape the limitations of your human condition. At first, you may find solace in organized religion, sensual love, external success, and power; or you may attempt to escape through addiction, self-harm, or even death.

However, these experiences invariably bring you back to the suffering you were trying to avoid until you have matured enough to realize that the freedom for which you long cannot be found outside of you—that the only way out of pain is *through* it, delving within to find its source and stepping out of the mental entrapment causing your soul to reincarnate. Once the desire to stop the wheel of *Samsara* is sparked, you initiate a transformation that begins by taking spiritual responsibility for your thoughts and actions. Even without the idea of karma or reincarnation, the repetitiousness of life produces this desire, which is Consciousness drawing you from within. This marks an internal shift in awareness that gradually uncovers what gets in the way of true happiness. All your struggles and limitations prod you toward this shift.

Each birth animates the false I-sense that gradually sets in motion tendencies, memories, and karmic ties from certain seeds of perception in your causal body; they start to bloom from conception and birth. Then your soul lands in the environment most conducive to energizing those imprints in need of resolution to eventually break free from the illusion and suffering of material reality. These become your main wounds and hurdles in life, as well as opportunities to dissolve the concepts that keep your negative aspects active. Past karma determines your circumstances and genetic content while your predominant tendencies get reflected through your interactions during the development of your ego.

The roles you take establish your place in the family on a subconscious level. Depending on your natural dispositions and the needs, expectations, and roles of other family members, you may be the caretaker, the black sheep, the favorite, the scapegoat, the outsider, the rescuer, the fixer, the weakly, the responsible or smart one, the pleaser, the average or "not good enough," the creative one, the entertainer, or a combination of these and other functions within the family. In addition, the positive and negative qualities of your causal seeds (*samskaras*) match those of the people you live and interact with, and this also determines your status in the group and in other groups later on.

There is a subtle exchange of energy that sets specific dynamics in motion through your interactions; you interpret these according to the causal seeds they activate in your perception. As a child, you are mainly focused on those you get attached and look up to, and your self-perception is shaped according to their reactions. You accept or suppress certain aspects in yourself depending on their needs and expectations, because you haven't yet developed the higher mind or had enough life experience to make your own choices. You are completely codependent; someone else has the power to make all the decisions regarding your life and behavior.

You reject what isn't acceptable as per cultural and family conditioning, adjusting your self-expression to fit in and avoid rejection or punishment. Family dynamics energize predominant, subconscious tendencies that translate as feeling more or less welcomed, loved, or visible than others. This creates specific dynamics with your parents, siblings, and those around you. But you are not a blank slate or a victim of circumstance, simply absorbing everyone else's stuff; you *share* positive and negative causal seeds and soul memories with the people in your life, especially with your parents or main authority figures.

If you didn't, the circumstances of your birth would have been different, since there would be no resonance with them. However, everyone reacts and individuates according to their predominant patterns of perception. So even if you share the same parents and environment, as well as similar circumstances and predispositions with your siblings and other people, your life unfolds in a particular, individualized manner. Your ego makes it a unique, self-centered mental movie.

The mind field is like a two-stream river. One stream flows toward the world of sensory objects, fueled by active tendencies; it appears as a continuous current of thoughts and desires. The other stream flows away from the world, toward the Inner Self, and grows with the seeds of virtuous actions, self-discipline, and dispassion. It is very easy to get pulled outward, because it is the natural direction of the ego-mind; the collective reality holds immense amounts of energy luring you with the promise of pleasure. In contrast, widening the inward stream requires an ongoing, resolute effort to liberate your soul from the suffering that usually follows worldly desires.

This divergence of the mind can also be seen as two aspects of the ego in your perception and experience of life. One is your *sense of self*, which allows you to make individual choices, walk a separate path, and pursue your soul's inherent drive for expression. The other is what I call your *sense of otherness*, which holds past family dynamics and socio-cultural conditioning reflecting the main issues you are here to resolve. It is easy to spot them in

Your Egoic Sense of Otherness

others while keeping them hidden from yourself, because this is the main aspect of your ego that constantly draws your attention outward to maintain the illusion of duality. In this context, your sense of otherness filters and colors your reality with unconscious, outdated beliefs about yourself that keep your negative tendencies active.

Now, your sense of self is still an aspect of ego, not your true Self, but it helps you steer the mind away from the world when you nurture the innate desire for individuation, self-expression, and freedom. It is your particular viewpoint or inner voice allowing you to become one-with-yourself as you search for the meaning and purpose of your life. However, your sense of otherness tends to overpower it by taking much more room in your perception, since it kicks in whenever you engage with the external reality through your interactions and goals. That is, anytime you are outwardly focused rather than anchored in yourself or looking within.

It is like a coat you are unaware of wearing that is woven with old mental and emotional patterns coloring your experience of life. It holds dynamics you internalized while your ego was developing in early childhood, in resonance with past seeds of perception. Now it distorts your current experiences by keeping you emotionally in the past. You have invested immense amounts of energy in it by focusing on other people since you were born, expecting gratification and validation from them. For this reason, it has acquired too much power and become an *inner bully* that sabotages your process of individuation and growth.

Taking over your consciousness, it keeps you from perceiving yourself except *through* or *in relation* to others: how they treat or judge you, how you compare to them, and whether you meet their expectations and they approve of your choices. It is mostly projected in your reality as "other people," although there is no real separation between you and others—just the illusion created by the ego-mind. As long as you believe that others are separate, rather than a reflection of your egoic sense of otherness, you will perpetuate the division that produces power dynamics, conflicts, and pain.

Arguing, fighting, or reacting to other people's choices makes your sense of otherness stronger, since you invest more emotional energy in it instead of recognizing it as the reflection of what you are here to resolve in yourself. The only way to diminish it, while transforming your reality in the process, is by nurturing your sense of self: listening to your inner voice and pursuing activities that anchor you in the present and make you feel good about yourself. That is, honoring your individual expression (the Best Version of You) instead of identifying with other people's behavior. This entails overcoming the emotional codependency of childhood you unconsciously recreate in your relationships. But as you balance the dominant aspect of ego that distorts your perception of reality, you gain emotional freedom, which is an important step toward spiritual freedom.

To make itself felt, the ego requires a distinction between subjective and objective reality—of self and *other*. As an individualizing principle, it cannot exist in the realm of sensory perception without the idea of *otherness*, because there can be no individuality except in relation to something other than *me*. Yet you have the power to direct your mind toward or away from the external world, where your sense of otherness is projected. Your sense of self yearns for authenticity and freedom of expression, while your sense of otherness keeps you focused on the world of appearances. Since both aspects of ego fight for space in your mental field, balancing this internal dynamic is crucial to create more *togetherness* and eventually reach Oneness.

Life is a play of Consciousness, a game of self-awareness. Your experiences show you what you need to resolve to reclaim your true nature. When you remove the self-centeredness of concepts such as *me* and *mine*, you can participate in the world while being fully present and engaged, like an actor in a play, without fixating on any of your roles. Consciousness plays hide-and-seek with itself, and you can either seek or hide from yourself as well. Your sense of self is a unique, albeit self-centered expression of the Self that gives rise to your sense of otherness as the world, which blurs the clarity of who you really are and actualizes the delusion of duality that produces suffering.

Your sense of self seeks individuation to transcend it, gradually maturing until it is ready to merge with the Self. For this reason, as I will explore in more detail, the key to your emotional and spiritual freedom is to *redirect your awareness from otherness to self.* Your self-perception is not the result of merely absorbing your childhood environment and responding to the expectations of those you loved, although these are important aspects in the formation of your ego. Your life is fueled by the predominant tendencies, beliefs, and desires in your causal body. You appear to internalize aspects of your parents, siblings, and other authority figures, but this is because you *share* certain causal seeds with them that get activated through your interactions. Your reality is shaped with your own subconscious content, so you are solely responsible for your experience of life.

As you get older, the type of relationships you establish also happen through resonance of similar or matching causal seeds, which creates dynamics that reflect your sense of otherness as something external. Owing to the shape-shifting, mobile quality of your ego, boundaries get blurry with guilt, pressure, or doubts that cause a misalignment between your subjective and objective reality. Your inner bully keeps hidden by drawing your attention outward—to *others*—in an attempt to stall your individuation and expression, as well as the desire to uncover deeper truths.

To use a popular term, your sense of otherness *gaslights* your sense of self. This is why it is easy to manipulate or get manipulated, no matter how smart you are. Your sense of otherness is always trying to manipulate you into believing yourself to be what isn't the real you. But you can learn to recognize and diminish it by taking full spiritual responsibility for everything in your life without falling prey to shame or blame, which keeps the inner bully in control. When balanced, this aspect turns into an internal support system that will also manifest externally. Now, how did it acquire such power as to distort your self-perception?

In early childhood, you expressed yourself with much love, enthusiasm, and curiosity. As you started learning what was acceptable and what wasn't, you began conforming in order to meet the expectations of those with any authority over you. While absorbing the outer world, you had to adjust your perception and behavior to avoid the pain of rejection or punishment. Their needs prevailed over yours, stressing the sense of separation from those with the power to provide or deny the love, nourishment, and care you needed to feel safe and develop a strong sense of self.

This, of course, is a gradual karmic process. As a baby, you are completely codependent, unable to survive on your own. There is no clear division between you and the world until you are more grounded in your body, and you express yourself openly if you are uncomfortable or hungry. Then your ego takes a more distinct form as your physical senses and mental functions start developing during the first seven-year cycle of life. Your status and roles within the groups to which you belong are established in resonance with your seeds of perception. How you experience and interpret family life shapes your sense of otherness, but you are still driven by and able to express your sense of self to some extent. If this is not possible because of a rigid environment, you are likely to hide or voice it in dysfunctional ways.

The second seven-year life cycle proves more puzzling. You are still very codependent and focused on other people's emotional energy and responses, now beyond your family circle, and you are also more aware of your physical body and the sense of separation through your interactions with others. Your consciousness of the outside world is increasing, along with your hormone levels, both of which magnify your confusion about individuating. You have to deal with internal and external changes, swinging between the desire for greater independence and the need for validation and support.

The intensity of your struggle hinges upon your past karma and active tendencies of perception, both of which are reflected through the level of emotional intelligence and freedom of expression in your environment. You may feel alone with your conflicts, you may act out your sense of isolation and the fear of change, or you may be subjected to your peers acting out theirs upon you. In other words, your sense of otherness is getting stronger and beginning to overpower your sense of self.

This continues into adolescence, or the third seven-year cycle, which can be quite a challenging transition. Increasing hormones bring more unexpected physical and emotional changes, further magnifying your identification with the body as well as the sense of separation. Life becomes confusing, and the demands of the outside world put a lot of pressure on you. Now you are more focused on your interactions with your peers as a source of validation; your sensory perception is getting stronger because of hormonal changes and an increasing flow of sensual desires from the ego-mind.

This may create anxiety and insecurity, since you are pulled in opposite directions: the safety of childhood against the craving for new experiences and individuation; the familiar past in contrast with the uncertainty of the future; the self you know and feel forced to leave behind competing with the self-images you are compelled to build to fit in with your peers. You look for comfort and support from your friends, thinking they are going through what you are going through, as opposed to your parents, who have a hard time accepting all your changes.

They struggle with your need for independence, for it highlights the loss of control over the younger version of you to which they are attached. Since your sense of self feels jeopardized, it defies your sense of otherness through conflicts that may escalate to destructive actions. Your reality reflects what is happening on a subconscious level: the hormonal changes, the physical and emotional confusion, the need to belong (now outside the family group), and the fear of losing yourself.

You believe that you must fight the restrictions of authority figures trying to squelch your individuality, when in reality you are striving to rescue a confused sense of self from an opposing sense of otherness exacerbated by hormones and increased social activity. If you are not able to integrate and be at peace with your changing needs, you simply project your confusion and the internalized dynamics of your upbringing onto other people while judging and rejecting them.

Rebelliousness is a natural aspect of this stage; it is an attempt to restore the internal balance between your individual needs and the pressure of social demands. Without guidance or self-awareness, however, the ego tends to incite anger as a defense mechanism, activating negative impulses toward harmful or self-destructive behaviors. Anxiety, depression, and other health issues may arise as unconscious expressions of guilt and self-punishment, as well as suppressed anger. At this point, a therapeutic, non-judgmental space, as well as creative activities for self-expression, can be your saving grace; your options, again, will depend on your individual tendencies and karma.

By the time you reach your fourth seven-year cycle, which marks the dawn of adulthood and greater independence, hormones have settled down to a certain extent and your sense of otherness has congealed. Now you cannot help but perceive yourself *through* others, seeking external validation and support as you set out to explore and find your place in the world. Your satisfaction relies mostly on relationships, since your sense of otherness overpowers your sense of self. You may easily lose yourself in them, giving your energy away while you strive to prove how right, special, or better you are by comparing yourself to other people.

At the end of this fourth cycle comes what is known in astrology as your Saturn Return, which is a transition of about two and a half years happening every twenty-eight to thirty years to initiate you into a new cycle of experience. It compels you to reassess your sense of self by questioning the structures you have relied upon until that point. Generally speaking, this is likely the first time you may seriously ask yourself, "Who am I?" and "What is the meaning and purpose of my life?" Depending on past choices, this period may bring a disruptive identity crisis, a wonderful awakening that propels you in search of a more authentic version of yourself, or a combination of both.

It often marks a turning point leading to your most intense karmic cycle as well. This is when you are expected to build a career, raise a family, accomplish your goals, and fulfill other worldly desires, all of which feeds on and reinforces your sense of otherness. It is not unusual to have existential crises during this cycle, since you are confronted with the limitations of physical reality and the aging process, as well as the challenge to balance your individual needs against those of other people. Saturn rules karma, so it brings your sense of otherness to the forefront as it transits your life.

Whenever your inner bully takes too much room in your perception, it pulls you into a *wounded child archetype* that feels anxious about the future, overwhelmed by decisions, or in temper-tantrum mode, resentful toward others, life itself, or God. It is easy to see that the world at large is emotionally stuck in this archetype. Most people are either scared, angry, or in conflict with one another because of past, unresolved emotions. This lack of maturity perpetuates suffering and imbalance in the realm of ego. The idea that peace will come from the outside, either from a certain group (an idealized family) or some type of savior or father figure, is one of the illusions of the wounded child hoping to be rescued or saved. Only when you delve within to dissolve your negative patterns can you experience peace, which will then be reflected in the external world.

You take responsibility for your own happiness when you recognize your false ideas and identifications. This process starts by viewing your sense of otherness as a relentless inner bully that makes you feel that *you should be someone other than who you are, doing something other than what you are doing (or would like to do)*. It robs you of the clarity to express yourself freely by trapping you in the past through an outdated, distorted self-perception.

This constant self-judgment pressures and pushes you off-center, deflating you with a sense of insufficiency based on absurd, imaginary standards of perfection. It is an ongoing mental chatter that gets activated when your attention is directed outward, raising fears and insecurities from the illusions and unresolved emotions of childhood. If you are not conscious of your wounded aspects, it is easy to get manipulated or scammed. Individuation demands self-awareness. Your sense of otherness will blur your clarity by holding you in patterns of emotional codependency, particularly when you take steps toward greater freedom on any level—from the past, from old, fixed roles, from harmful behaviors, from situations in which you feel trapped, or from toxic relationships.

Besides the negative chatter of your inner bully, the most obvious reflection of your sense of otherness is, well, through *others*. It may show up as opposition, judgments, expectations, blame, deceit, or anything that pulls you to the past with old feelings such as being alone, invisible, unheard, rejected, wrong, left out, powerless, not good enough, and so on. The ego-mind can and will use any negative emotion to start a snowball that takes you down a rabbit hole. It is most obvious when you start pursuing a desire. You think you deserve the object of your desire, but the *emotional message* you receive through the attitudes and reactions of other people is the opposite of what you want, making you *feel* that you are doing something wrong and should drop your desire.

It does not matter whether it is unreasonable, unfair, hidden, or outspoken; if your reality triggers negative emotions, it means that your wounded child archetype has taken over your perception. Other people don't even have to go directly against you; they may simply ignore you or respond from fear or guilt that has nothing to do with you. They may, willingly or unwillingly, create obstacles and disruptions that make you deviate from your goals. Unresolved emotions can be aroused in innumerable ways, because it is not other people causing them; people are just vehicles of your sense of otherness reflecting the distorted self-perception that you are here to heal.

Through your identification with the body and mind, the ego keeps you enslaved to the delusion of *otherness*, making it appear as something external and separate from you. It pushes the belief that your happiness depends on what others do or say in regard to your individual expression. This becomes clear if you start watching where and how you invest your energy, and what your conversations revolve around. Are they about other people or the past, or are they about your ideas, projects, goals, and spiritual aspirations in the present? Do you do or say things expecting external validation, or do you do them for the sake of self-expression? In other words, is your experience of life about *you* or about *others*?

You cannot diminish your sense of otherness until you comprehend that nothing in your life is really separate from you; that you are your life, the space where everything happens. People and objects appear separate because the ego individualizes all forms and creates the illusion of duality, but they are appearances in the Pure Awareness you are. To transform your reality into a more enjoyable journey, you must take full spiritual responsibility for everything in it to break free from outdated patterns of perception that keep revolving in your mind. Real change can only happen from within, because your life is a soul-guided journey of self-discovery, a mental movie or dream within the dream of Consciousness through which you reclaim your eternal Self.

***

Radical Honesty Process

Truth is the main goal of a spiritual seeker. Just like negative karma often starts by deviating from the truth, inner peace also begins with honesty. You have to be honest with yourself to be honest with anyone else, by freeing yourself from an excessive sense of otherness that inhibits your inner voice. Being honest is not about sharing everything, proving something, or imposing your views; it is about knowing yourself—the good, the bad, and the ugly in you. It requires ongoing self-reflection, for the ego-mind veils your negative patterns at every opportunity.

I shared this exercise in a previous publication,[1] but I am giving a slightly modified version here to help you uncover how your sense of otherness distorts your perception. Do it whenever you get triggered by unpleasant situations, but try to focus on a single issue at a time to avoid getting sidetracked. Follow each step as best as you can, using your own words and experiences.

---

[1] This exercise and the one at the end of Chapter Six (Retrieving Your Little Orphans) were first published in *The Indigo Journals: Spiritual Healing For Indigo Adults & Other Feminine Souls*, Sri Devi Press, 2015.

1. WHAT is the main ISSUE and the EMOTIONS you are experiencing right now?

Describe one specific issue you would like to explore, along with the negative emotions it stirs up. Examples: "I don't feel supported by my partner (friend, family member, colleague) and it makes me angry (frustrated, resentful, discouraged)." "I am not appreciated by my spouse (mate, boss, child), which makes me feel invisible (small, unheard, insignificant, useless)." "I get insecure (anxious, awkward, judgmental, defensive) when I meet someone I consider more attractive (intelligent, successful, powerful)." "I feel incompetent (embarrassed, a failure) because I cannot finish any of the projects I start." "I feel rejected and alone when others don't do what I want or things don't go the way I expect." "I get anxious and overwhelmed if I have to make a decision on my own or do something just for myself." "I don't deserve to enjoy life (succeed, be happy, be at peace) when I see others (my parents, siblings, friends, partner) unhappy or suffering." "I feel wrong or guilty for what I did (or said) if others did not agree with me."

2. WHERE does this come from and WHO does it involve?

Your issues originate in impressions from childhood, which is when your predominant causal seeds started blooming. Think of the main person(s) with whom you would associate this issue as a child, remembering situations where you felt the same way, going back as far as you can. Examples: "It makes me think of the way my father (mother, sibling, grandparent) reacted when this or that happened." "It reminds me of my mother or father dismissing my efforts, favoring my sibling(s), or comparing me to others." "It is similar to how my mother (father, grandparent, sibling) used to make me feel wrong (insignificant, ashamed, not good enough, unheard) whenever I tried to express myself." "It reminds me of my brother (sister, father, mother, teacher) humiliating me in front of other people or bullying me to get what they wanted."

3. WHAT is the hidden PAYOFF of your ego/sense of otherness that makes you hold on to this?

This is the core element of this exercise. Keep in mind that the payoff of your ego is what preserves the imbalance between your sense of self and your sense of otherness. It is never something positive for you, since it keeps the ego-mind in control of your perception. But it is a hidden motivation of some kind—something you don't want to see in yourself. It maintains a distorted self-perception by skirting around the truth, either because the truth is painful or it jeopardizes your illusions and self-images. The key is to uncover the beliefs that keep your sense of otherness directing your behavior. Since it traps you in the past, *its hidden payoff goes against real individuation and freedom*, triggering resistance to grow out of your wounded child archetype and perpetuating outdated, codependent patterns of perception and behavior.

Examples of the egoic payoff are: "I feel safe in my comfort zone, even if it is constrictive." "I avoid fear, guilt, or being judged by pleasing or giving my power to other people." "It is easier or safer to hide behind others." "If I stay small and invisible, I don't need to make any effort or risk failing." "I don't have to take responsibility for myself if I take emotional responsibility for others." "I symbolically hold my parents accountable for failing me by being angry, unhappy, or a victim." "I can hide my fears and insecurities by focusing on and judging other people." "I remain loyal to my family by staying small, unhappy, or fixed in the roles I took as a child to be accepted." "I can avoid seeing my shortcomings if I blame others for my feelings." "Controlling others with anger or guilt makes me feel less vulnerable."

4. WHY are you AFRAID of letting this go?

What would happen if you stopped reinforcing the payoff of your ego and the outdated beliefs that feed it? Who (in your past) would you be going against or being disloyal to, and how? Transforming your hidden motivations entails letting go of the fixed roles and attitudes that keep you stuck in an outdated self-perception. Since your sense of otherness reflects these internal figures and voices, it turns into resistance, and you have to dig deeply to move past it.

Here are some examples: "I'd be afraid that something bad would happen and I'd be punished." "I'd end up alone, rejected, or not knowing where I belong." "I'd feel too guilty because I am supposed to make others happy." "I'd be disloyal to my mother, father, siblings because they were/are unhappy, unfortunate, poor, ill, codependent, etc." "I'd be perceived as selfish or useless if I didn't put other people's needs and feelings before mine." "I'd have to make too many changes to let go of what feels familiar and safe." "I'd lose my sense of purpose without taking responsibility for those I am attached to." "I'd have to look closely at myself and do something about my illusions and flaws." "I'd have to end my relationship(s) or reinvent myself."

Notice how your sense of otherness produces fear of change with thoughts of becoming a bad person or losing something important if you take spiritual responsibility for yourself instead of fixating on others. First of all, none of these thoughts are necessarily true. Also, life is not about being good or bad, loyal or disloyal, according to some outdated ideas, but about reclaiming the freedom to express who you are—what makes you a unique expression of Consciousness. The key is disbelieving the ego-mind that creates labels to distort your experiences with the delusion of duality. The fear of change, or the unknown, deters you from turning inward to let go of the beliefs that keep you in the past, secretly seeking validation. However, when you look within and nurture your sense of self, you spontaneously become more loving and compassionate, opening up to new possibilities of experience.

5. WHAT other negative BELIEFS about yourself does it reflect or maintain?

Observe how your statements express the way you perceive yourself *in relation to others*, and uncover what is underneath them: what unconscious beliefs do they uphold or justify in your current reality? Some examples: "I am not good, smart, attractive, or successful enough." "I am worthless and need external approval to be valuable." "I am insignificant, since there is always something or someone more important than me." "I cannot trust or deserve my own power." "I am responsible for other people's emotions and reactions." "I need to be controlled, limited, or silenced to hide and feel safe." "I need to be needed, useful, responsible, or perfect to be loved." "I don't deserve to express myself, accomplish my goals, fulfill my desires, have loving relationships, enjoy life, be free."

Notice that the statements in this exercise are meant to help you take responsibility for your self-perception. Also, note how none of them are really true; they are false ideas woven into patterns of self-perception you have carried for a long time without investigating their validity. They reflect the past and not who you are or what you want *now*. Now you have gained enough life experience to question them, so that you can be more objective and discern the truth within.

6. Now FORGIVE yourself and others, and LET GO!

Once you uncover your ego's payoff, the self-defeating beliefs keeping it in place, and the part you have unconsciously played in the dynamics that are causing you pain, ask yourself: "Am I ready to release this issue, forgiving myself and those involved in it—both in the past and in my current reality—to open up to new possibilities of experience?" If you are ready, you can just drop those negative beliefs right then and there. Once you see yourself clearly, it is as simple as making the choice to let go, even if it warrants the grief of recognizing your own lack of love. If you don't feel ready yet, then go through the process again until you do, for the sake of your own freedom.

Disempowering beliefs keep the ego in charge simply because they are familiar and repetitive. They have accumulated a lot of energy, so it takes an emotional effort to release them. You must learn to "ride the wave of discomfort" that arises when you choose to nurture your sense of self; it is unconscious guilt trying to deter you from going against the inertial direction of your past. Guilt is the opposite of freedom, and fear is the opposite of love, so the ego pushes them to disconnect you from your true nature. Make the decision to be radically honest with yourself from now on, to develop the self-awareness, discipline, and discrimination needed to master the ego-mind!

CHAPTER SIX

The Mental Movie You Call Your Life

Just as the spider emits the thread (of the web) out of itself and again withdraws it into itself, likewise the mind projects the world out of itself and again resolves it into itself. When the mind comes out of the Self, the world appears.
— *Ramana Maharshi*

A young cowherd takes his family cattle to the meadows every morning. He brings them back to the shed at the end of the day, tying them up to individual posts to prevent them from roaming about at night. One evening, as he is going through his routine, he notices one of the cows is missing her rope. Unable to find a new one, he runs to his neighbor for advice. The man instructs him to pretend to tie the cow, making sure the animal sees him do it. The boy follows the instructions, using an imaginary rope to fasten the cow to a post.

In the morning, while he is letting the cattle out, the boy sees that cow standing still in the same spot as the night before. He tries to coax her to join the herd, but the animal won't budge. Perplexed, he rushes to consult his neighbor again. This time the man says, "The cow believes to be tied up. Now you must pretend to untie her." Once the boy mimics the movements of loosening up the invisible rope, the cow happily leaves the shed.

The cow believes that she is tethered because she has been tied before, so she expects it. Similarly, as long as the ego-mind is in control of your perception, you experience repetitive situations colored by revolving mental patterns woven together with thoughts, emotions, memories, and actions, because you have identified with them, even if they are outdated or untrue. The ego-mind actualizes ingrained impressions and tendencies in your causal body and then keeps you spinning in them. This revolving principle applies to all aspects of Creation through the elements and qualities of nature shaping cycles within cycles in the eternal dream of Consciousness.

Some of these are enormous, universal periods lasting hundreds of thousands of years, such as the Age of Darkness or *Kali Yuga*, which humanity has been undergoing and will continue to experience for many more thousands of years. Within it, there are shorter cosmic cycles that are still thousands of years long. In this dualistic, bipolar universe, we are reaching the end of a masculine cycle (action- and ego-oriented), shifting toward a feminine one meant to bring balance on the planet—that is, of course, until it reaches its end and a new masculine cycle begins. Then there are smaller cycles, such as astrological ages and planetary transits, and much shorter ones like the years, seasons, months, days, hours, and minutes within a lifespan.

Like the gears of a finely crafted clock, these regular changes keep everything in motion and expansion within the cosmic play. The natural stages of development, maturity, and decline repeat at every level of experience as well. You go through lifetimes and periods within each lifetime of greater activity or more intense contemplation, depending on your causal seeds, priorities, and function within the cosmic dream. Your soul journey unfolds through cycles of evolution or outward experience and involution or introspection to learn about yourself from the choices you make. The key to a graceful adventure is moving through the changes without getting stuck or spinning for too long in lower mental states. In practical terms, it is a matter of recognizing your unconscious patterns as they revolve throughout your life, dismissing those that cause pain.

On the outside, things have improved and continue to progress in relation to previous stages. Scientific, technological, and social advancements have created better conditions and new avenues for development. Below the surface, however, not much has changed; humanity is still experiencing suffering, injustice, and inequality, because the world is a creation of the ego with its inherent tendency toward division, conflict, and the craving for control. Likewise, the scenarios and people in your life may change, but your perception is tainted with what is underneath the appearances: past impressions, unresolved emotions, and so on. That is because you believe that you are your story—your past—rather than who you are right here, right now.

You identify with your mind, which is a collection of mental impressions and memories, and with your body, the vehicle through which those memories are experienced and expressed. Since your life emerges when the light of Consciousness is projected onto your mind, and your experience is filtered through the sensory perception of your subtle and causal bodies, it is clear that your experience of reality is a mental projection of the past. But it is also a portal into your subconscious offering ongoing opportunities for awareness and healing, so that you may leave the past behind, where it belongs, and be fully present, anchored in the moment.

You are the Pure Awareness where everything appears and disappears, although the ego-mind blurs this truth by making things and people seem separate from you. The first step to remove this false perception of reality is accepting things as they play out, surrendering to life *as it is*, instead of expecting people and things to be something they are not to meet your needs. When you let go of your illusions, you effect a spontaneous transformation without forcing anything.

As a projection of the ego, the world tends to be on a painful, destructive course, but the pain you see on the outside comes from your own entrapment. There is no real separation between you and others; it is a mirage created by the ego-mind, which is the Self experiencing itself in an individualized, human form. You can attempt to diminish the sorrow you witness and encounter with love and compassion, but you also need to trust that it is a divine play where everything happens on its own, as it is meant to happen. You could spend lifetimes trying to fix the world or you can just make the effort to find the source of your projection to break free from it.

Until that happens, your life is an ongoing battle between two conflicting yet parallel forces of Consciousness: the pure *I-am-ness* at the core of your existence and the ego that hijacks it with identifications such as "I am this or that," which disconnect you from the blissful presence of simply *being*. At the level of your ego consciousness, it becomes an internal battle between your sense of self and your sense of otherness aiming for the control of your perception. But behind it all is the light of the Supreme Self. Without it, you wouldn't be conscious of the world; and without your ego, you wouldn't perceive it the way you do—as separate, external objects, there to fulfill your desires.

In my analogy of the Supreme Soul being the ocean, the Inner Self being the seawater, and your individual soul being the water trapped in a bottle, bumping into other bottles, the ego-mind is the illusory container skewing the truth that there is no difference between you, others, or Consciousness; that the water outside is the same infinite ocean as the water inside. Although people and objects in your mental field are filtered through your sense of otherness, you are your life. You are the subtle cause of it as it happens in your mind, and no one else can perceive it from your unique viewpoint. Furthermore, since your mind is a collection of memories and impressions, and you perceive life according to your predominant tendencies, it is clear that your external reality is an individualized mental movie through which you can know yourself. That is, *a projection of the past where things appear to be but aren't really separate from you.*

If you watch a good movie, you get immersed in it, relating to the characters and going through all sorts of emotions, as if you were part of the plot. But you are always aware that it is a fictional projection on a screen. You remain a detached spectator and don't mistake the projection of images for your reality, even if they appear very real and tangible. You also appreciate that, although the situations and people in it seem to occur in the present—when you are watching the movie—they have been frozen in time, imprinted on a photographic film or digital file.

Despite its three-dimensional appearance, what is showing on the screen is not happening in the same space-time as the audience viewing it; it is a virtual reality. The same can be said of a dream, although dreams tend to be more chaotic or disjointed, because the conscious mind that fashions a logical structure recedes to give way to a free stream of memories, desires, and fears symbolically woven with your imagination. A movie follows an organized, well-crafted script that has a clear direction, but in the dream state the conscious mind isn't there to judge or control what is happening. And yet, you perceive things as vividly in your dreams as in a movie or your everyday life.

While you are dreaming, a variety of scenarios, characters, and stories appear without contact with the outside world or the physical senses. The content emerges from the subconscious, and sometimes also from the superconscious dimensions of your soul. When you wake up, you can dismiss your dreams as fiction or you can analyze them to better understand yourself. When you are in the wakeful state, you are also projecting past impressions, memories, and desires from within, but they crystalize as tangible situations through your sensory perception. The ego-mind organizes them within the idea of space-time and you think of them as *your* experiences.

Everything appears on the screen of your mind. You observe it from your *I-am-ness*, which is the constant sense of being you. Since you are aware of participating in your life, you believe yourself to be the one consciously creating this personal movie. However, as I have explained before, the mind is unconscious, like a screen or a receptacle of light. Your life unfolds on its own, just like your dreams, according to the *gunas* in your mind that reflect your past karma, impressions, and unfulfilled desires, in resonance with all the other appearances of Consciousness you are meant to encounter.

By coloring your perception, the ego-mind controls your behavior and experiences, preventing you from recognizing your personal life-movie as a dream within a dream. It veils a clear, undistorted access to your reality by tainting it with unresolved emotional energy and outdated patterns that revolve through your sense of otherness. It is like being trapped in a recurrent dream where the scenarios change but the emotional reactions remain the same until you realize you have been imagining different versions of the same dream and you start questioning it to discover new possibilities of experience.

In deep meditative or superconscious states, ordinary consciousness disappears along with the world. Even if you think the collective dream continues, it does not exist when you are not participating in it and there is no ego to experience it. It all emerges with you, including the idea that the world goes on without you. By the same token, you cannot realize your true Self unless you pierce through your identification with sensory perception as you observe your reality and mental-emotional fluctuations. You may get insightful glimpses every now and then, but as a spiritual seeker, your ultimate goal is to abide in the Self, seeing the cosmic dream for what it is, with the same attitude toward the world as when you watch a fictional film.

On the material plane, the mind is engaged through the physical senses that perceive things as solid and tangible, but this is due to the projection of previous impressions and contrasting variations of light in the mental movie appearing as your reality. Since it emerges from within you, you are the main character in your life-movie, and everything revolves around you as you interact with other people, who are also projecting and navigating their own life-movies.

Because of karmic resonance and subconscious collective needs, individual movies intersect at different points and levels through pleasant and painful exchanges. Again, these are different appearances of Consciousness in the field of Consciousness, but the ego-mind turns them into individualized experiences. Since the interactions between you and other people are invariably colored with past impressions, it is important to understand that the intersections with other movies reflect aspects that *mirror* your sense of otherness.

If you approach life as a journey of self-discovery, then any situation becomes an opportunity for greater awareness. You can only experience things as you, since only you can live your life. There is no difference, although you see it as something external because of the projection of your sense of otherness as *others*. It is like looking in the mirror and believing that there are two people looking at each other. Once you recognize it as your projection, you can use it to know yourself and heal the distortions of your self-perception—the source of your suffering. The people and events in your life are expressions of Consciousness helping you observe and know yourself, and you play a similar function for them as well.

Without self-awareness, all you see is your ego filtering and tainting your movie. You need to see yourself clearly to be able to see anyone else without the coloring of outdated beliefs and impressions. But to see yourself clearly, you have to uncover your patterns of perception. They won't magically disappear if you deny or rationalize them, or if you fixate on regrets from so-called mistakes and failures, which are just experiences to help you learn about yourself. You must unravel and starve negative patterns as they cycle time and again in your life, until they go to sleep. You gain emotional maturity through this process, so situations that may have been overwhelming in the past become much smaller.

It takes discipline and perseverance to transform your mental habits. Subconscious impressions can fuel a positive or negative response to a seemingly unrelated event, if it activates old causal seeds. Past events no longer exist, yet their imprints color your life-movie now, so an emotional effort is required to stay in the present rather than blindly following the impulses of the ego-mind. No matter how old or recent, how conscious or unconscious your memories may be, the past can only be resolved in the present, for nothing is real but the present.

This is a play of Consciousness, a game of self-awareness, where the goal is to become conscious of yourself until you realize you are Consciousness—One with everything and everyone. What makes you suffer is your imaginary identification with the body and mind. The idea of being a "person" separate from other "persons" pinches you out of the Oneness or totality of the Self. This is why you yearn for it in the union, communion, and *togetherness* with others like you.

Owing to the egoism and spiritual ignorance of the ego-mind, however, you expect people to behave according to *your* needs, while everyone else is trying to figure out their life-movie and expecting you to behave according to *their* needs as well. This sets the typical power dynamics that dominate most relationships, in overt and subtle ways. If you perceive yourself and engage with the world through your sense of otherness, you will seek love and validation through other people rather than recognizing that you are the love you have been looking for. You may unwillingly sabotage your relationships with illusions, demands, and resentments from past unfulfilled desires instead of forming mature partnerships.

If you pay close attention, you will notice that certain aspects repeat over and over in your movie through your interactions: you take on the same roles, expect the same things, and struggle with or fight about the same issues. You can blame everyone else for your frustration, but these are old, revolving patterns that reflect the internal dynamics between your sense of self and your sense of otherness. The repetitiousness may bring you to a point of saturation where you start craving greater freedom, but, of course, for anything to change, you have to transform your self-perception, which is what shapes your experiences. Once you recognize your life-movie as a reflection of the past, you can resolve what it is showing you about yourself that keeps bringing situations you no longer want.

Your own tendencies keep you going in an inertial direction, reinforcing outdated beliefs, but your soul is trying to nudge you in the opposite direction to balance karmic dynamics while incorporating what you have previously learned. In this process of integration, new desires and goals propel you forward while old patterns hold you back with resistance. You are likely to follow the familiar orientation of the past unless you make the effort to complete a U-turn by letting go of outdated tendencies of thought and behavior. This takes great self-awareness, honesty, and courage. Most people start turning in a new direction when they find pain or difficulties, but they often stop as soon as things seem better, before completing a full turn.

It seems easier to wait for things to change from the outside rather than making what is unconscious conscious. You may think, "If I had more of this or that," or "If this person would behave this or that way," or "If things were like this or that, then I'd be happy." Once you comprehend that your life is your own projection, it is obvious that this perspective can never bring you what you yearn for. Only *you* can transform your movie from within. The reward is your freedom, as you discover new dimensions of life.

Your journey is already set, just not in a fixed or rigid manner, given that life itself is fluid. Your road map is designed by past karma, in synchronistic resonance with other souls. You can either navigate it fighting and resisting what you don't like, thus creating more pain, or you can embrace it by surrendering to what is. This depends on your level of maturity and humility, and on how strong is your desire to reclaim your eternal Self. That is, where you are at on the Love-Consciousness Pyramid.

There is no way to predict when, how, or why the seeds of past, virtuous choices will sprout to bring deeper clarity or insight. Your job is to purify the mind of ego, which is what produces desires for sensory gratification, sabotaging the discipline needed for spiritual growth. Your life-movie unfolds as a projection of your causal seeds of perception, so the key is observing it with enough detachment to discern the main three aspects it is always pointing at through your sense of otherness: *what you need to let go of, what you need to nurture, and what you need to develop—in yourself.*

By gaining self-awareness, you can make decisions guided by clarity and love instead of the usual feelings of deficiency from your wounded child archetype. Anything you judge or resist on the outside usually reflects something you are trying to hide from yourself. As you nurture your sense of self, embracing and balancing the aspects that make you a unique human expression of Consciousness, you become more and more emotionally free. Then you achieve spiritual freedom, which is freedom from ego, when you completely surrender to the flow of life, accepting it without reservation while cultivating dispassion for the world that mirrors the ego-mind. At any level of freedom, the key ingredient is detachment or non-attachment.

For example, when a relationship comes to an end, you may swing between sadness, anger, guilt, doubt, and yearning for what was or could-have-been as you grieve and let go. Depending on the depth of your attachment, it may take months or years to get to a place of stability. If you happen to interact with the other person during this process, old unresolved emotions circle back around, often taking over your mental state. They pull you into the past, making you feel conflicted or uncomfortable. But those encounters gradually turn less triggering as your attachment fades away, until you reach a steady neutral state. In this case, you have strengthened your sense of self by reducing your sense of otherness; this is emotional freedom, which is expressed as independence, self-love, and self-care.

Spiritual freedom comes from dissolving all of the ego to turn the mind-body into a pure vessel of Consciousness, without feelings of *me* and *mine* or concepts of being separate from "another." The sense of doership and ownership disappears to give way to dispassion as you drop your identifications with the mind-body. To achieve this, you have to take responsibility for everything in your life-movie, recognizing it as an individualized projection that traps you in a self-centered dream. You awaken from the dream by clearing a false self-perception to make room for the love and light you essentially are.

True love is the absolute absence of fear, and true freedom is the absence of guilt. Since both *love* and *freedom* have been tainted with the usual distortions of *otherness*, it is best to think of them as inner peace—a pure state of contentment in the neutrality of simply *being*, where there is no self-centeredness or sense of separation. This is your deepest yearning: to feel anchored in the present moment, effortlessly connected to the flow of life, which is where your Inner Self abides. By cultivating the attitude of *non-action*—which comes from mindfulness, not apathy—the idea of being the doer or owner of your actions vanishes, along with the karma attached to them, as well as the fluctuations of the ego-mind dwelling in the past or worrying about the future.

However, this neutrality is what the ego-mind resists the most, because it doesn't want to stop being the owner of your mind, your body, and your actions, constantly luring you into experiences of pleasure and pain. As long as your mind is disturbed, all you can see is your ego tainting your reality with past emotional energy in need of resolution. Your individual road map and destiny are set, but the ego cannot accept this and clings to the illusion of control by pushing you off-center to sabotage any attempt to break free from it.

This becomes acutely obvious when you try to establish a meditation practice, since the mind bombards you with myriad thoughts to disrupt your endeavor. Your daily life isn't that different; you just don't notice how noisy your mind is unless you try to quiet it down. Likewise, whenever you take a step toward greater empowerment or freedom, your inner bully gets in the way to block you with doubts, fears, and all sorts of obstacles through your sense of otherness. It is relentless. You have to learn to manage your energy and pierce through your resistance to keep going, which is much easier when you uncover what your reality is pointing at in yourself.

That is what this book is all about. I want you to have both an intellectual understanding and a practical system to take full spiritual responsibility for your life-movie, so that it may lead you to inner peace. The process starts by embracing every aspect of your life as a reflection of conscious and unconscious choices made through your identification with sensory perception. In a nutshell, accepting that:

- Nobody is responsible for your happiness but you—not in this moment, not in the past, and not in the future.

- Nobody is to blame or at fault for anything, since there are no mistakes, only experiences from which you can learn.

- Nobody is going to fix things, for there is nothing to fix. You are the journey and the destination; everything you go through brings you closer to your true Self.

- Nobody is going to save you or take your negative karma away; it unfolds through your perception to help you remove what blocks the Pure Awareness you are.

- Your life is a mental projection happening within you: a personalized movie only you can transform and transcend by dismissing false, distorted ideas about yourself.

The key is your willingness to give up your identifications, but even that willingness belongs to the Divine. It is through Grace that you experience the world as well as the desire to rise above your suffering. Without Grace, there is no awareness or liberation. You suffer the consequences of your actions to know yourself and resolve the codependent fixation on others as separate from you. Where there is duality, there is conflict, imbalance, and power dynamics. Transcending your human condition demands breaking free from your ego—relinquishing your self-centered illusion of control to the Inner Self, the real director of your life.

* * *

Retrieving Your Little Orphans

This is a practice that will help you nurture your sense of self by integrating neglected yet essential aspects of your individual expression. In childhood, certain traits were considered unacceptable if they didn't meet the expectations or needs of those around you—that is, their own sense of otherness. Your ego created mechanisms to suppress these aspects, to avoid punishment, rejection, or anxiety, but they remained in your subconscious, yearning for freedom.

If you felt judged or criticized or not nurtured by the people you looked up to, then it is likely that most, if not all of your loving, curious, playful, enthusiastic, free, creative, intuitive, and spirited nature either got squelched or boxed into specific roles to meet family dynamics. In other words, you stopped loving chunks of yourself if other people didn't foster them, and you may still be doing this. I call them your *little orphans* because it is easier to reintegrate orphaned aspects through specific memories of younger versions of you. They hold negative emotions you have felt in the past, such as fear, shame, and loneliness. When you reclaim these fragments of your sense of self, you strengthen your inner voice, balance the excess *otherness* in your perception, and become one-with-yourself.

Whenever negative emotions come up, go inward and ask yourself, *"What am I feeling right now?"* Acknowledge what you are feeling for what it is: confusion, fear, anger, anxiety, sadness, envy, despair, frustration, etc. Don't push, justify, or rationalize it, trying to explain why you feel the way you do; simply acknowledge and accept it, without fixating on other people. Remember, focusing on others is what your sense of otherness will always push you to do, to prevent you from looking within. Then tune in with your heart to explore, "When have I experienced these feelings before?"

Let the trail of emotional memories take you through all the times you have felt what you are feeling now. Then use your creative imagination to connect with one or more orphans of yours—that is, one or more memories of yourself that you associate with these feelings. Go as far back as you can, but don't worry if you cannot reach your early childhood; just tune in with the orphans you are able to remember at the time. The more you practice, the further back your memory will stretch.

Approach them with compassion, letting them know that you are there for them and that you want to hear what they have to say. The crucial aspect here is to *give them a voice*, not to explain things or tell them how to feel or be. Inquire about what is going on around them and how they feel about it. Tell them they are not alone, and you want them to be part of your life now. Then just *listen*. There is no processing here, only recalling and intuitively expressing your *emotional* memories.

Even if you don't remember the exact context with mental images, you can rely on your intuition to guide you. After all, you have felt this way many, many times before. Also, trust the process without judging whether it is real or not, or whether it makes sense or not. This is not about logic; it is the retrieval of your inner voice and the aspects you have left behind. You are simply using your creative imagination to acknowledge and reclaim some of the energy that got stuck and keeps you in the past. That is, you are mothering yourself instead of expecting others to give you your voice. If you don't listen to yourself, nobody else will.

Visualize and talk to your little orphans with the same kindness and compassion you would show a young child who is afraid, sad, confused, or lonely. They have been overwhelmed and overpowered, perhaps even abused, so it may take some time for them to express things freely. Be patient and keep at it. If writing is easier, write loving letters to your little orphans and let the answers come to you as automatic writing. But remember, you are not the adult guiding or directing them in any way. Even if your intentions are good, they've had plenty of that already! It is not about explaining or trying to fix anything either, since you cannot change the past; your job is to simply listen to tune in and free your inner voice.

THE SWAN METHOD: FROM OTHERNESS TO SELF

CHAPTER SEVEN

Reclaiming Your Inner Power

As long as the mind is disturbed by desire, fear, pleasure and pain, it sees nothing but itself in everything. In other words, everything on the outside is our mind in a disturbed state. When it is not disturbed, there is perfect peace, and the disciple (mind) is liberated from the web of ignorance.
— *Baba Hari Dass*

In the *Mahabharata*, one of the greatest Indian epics symbolizing our internal battle with the negative tendencies of the ego, master Dronacharya decides to test his students in the art of archery. After hanging a wooden bird from a tree branch, he calls them outside, instructing them to aim for the bird's eye without shooting until he gives the go-ahead.

Once all the students are in position and all bows pointing at the target, the teacher approaches each individually, inquiring, "What do you see?" One by one, they say they can see the sky, the clouds, the tree, some branches, and other things surrounding the wooden figure. The only exception is Arjuna, who tells his guru the only thing he sees is the bird's eye.

This intensity of focus makes Arjuna an outstanding archer. His body and mind are perfectly synchronized. His bow is an extension of his body and his body an extension of his mind. He has no doubts, hesitation, or distractions hindering the resolve to reach his intended aim; this single-pointed attention excludes everything else. When the teacher gives him permission to shoot, his arrow goes straight into the bird's eye.

Arjuna represents the concentration of a pure mind. Here, purity of mind refers to the dissolution of ego leading to spiritual freedom. This is why concentration (*dharana*) is the limb in the yoga system that immediately precedes meditation; without complete focus, the mind wanders off, bombarding you with all sorts of thoughts that prevent you from reaching states of higher consciousness. Meditation is not just concentration but the uninterrupted flow of concentration on a single object (the breath, a mantra, a prayer, an image, a focal point, etc.), which eventually causes the mind to merge with that object.

The term *concentration* also refers to the increase in strength that results from removing any diluting agents in a substance. If you want to achieve anything in life, you have to stay focused and not leave room for distractions or doubts. Whether it is working on a personal or professional project, achieving a goal, creating something, or seeking spiritual enlightenment, success demands commitment, continuity, and single-mindedness. Furthermore, you cannot experience fulfillment without being fully engaged in what you are doing. Like Arjuna, you need to become one with your aim, centered and completely *present* in your endeavor, no matter how small or trivial.

The feeling of being anchored in yourself, undeterred by the ego-mind trying to pull you into the past or push you into the future, is empowering in itself. The opposite is also true. There is no real satisfaction when you are not connected to the flow of your life here and now. It doesn't matter if what you go through is pleasant or unpleasant; what makes a difference is whether you accept it or you resist it; whether you embrace the experience fully, you go through it half-heartedly, or you give up in the process, leaving it unfinished.

For instance, a partnership may break at some point, but if you have been present, committed, and self-aware, when it ends you naturally feel grief but also a sense of completion; you are ready for what comes next. A deeper engagement allows you to see the value of your experience, because it provides you with greater clarity about who you are: what you like and dislike, what brings you joy or pain, and what connects or disconnects you from yourself, which allows you to make more conscious choices.

Naturally, you suffer when things come to an end, but the grieving process may also lead to an inner transformation. For your sense of otherness, however, the end of a relationship usually means some kind of "failure" that reactivates imprints of rejection or guilt, as well as regrets and resentments. If you process your feelings by viewing your pain as the result of your own attachments and expectations, you can learn about yourself, while integrating the past, without dragging negative emotions to sabotage the experience of future relationships.

You reinforce your inner bully when you hold grudges or regrets about so-called mistakes and failures. Whether positive or painful, these are just *experiences* leading you on your journey to know yourself, which is the real purpose of life. With self-reflection, you can understand the meaning of the events in your personal and develop emotional and spiritual maturity. At some point, the need for sensory experiences will give way to a deeper yearning for inner peace, which is the magnetic pull of the Self. Surrendering to it demands humility and mental discipline, because your sense of otherness is continuously distracting you with the external world and setting you off-center with desires and negative emotions.

Where your attention goes, your energy and power follow. As long as the ego-mind controls your perception, it is easy to lose yourself in *otherness* without realizing how you have been giving and continue to give your power away—to your social environment, to people with any authority (real or imaginary), to those you are attracted to or care for, to those you blame for your afflictions, to unpleasant circumstances and painful memories, and even to disturbing news. This is how you let your sense of otherness take all the room in your movie while you shrink into a corner, feeling small. You regain your power by staying centered in the present, watching the drama your ego-mind funnels without identifying with it.

If you comprehend that nothing is really personal or belongs to you—since it is all a play of Divine Consciousness, and you are an expression of it, like everyone else—you unburden yourself from the sense of ownership that blocks the infinite potential of your soul. This freedom is the true power that uncovers the un-reality of the ego-mind you believe yourself to be. To deter you, however, the ego triggers unconscious fear and guilt creating many forms of resistance. It may show up as feelings of anxiety, pressure, or restlessness that keep you off-center; as anger or arguments with loved ones and coworkers; as injuries and illnesses; as sudden family or financial dramas, and so on. These situations may seem unrelated, but they reflect your resistance to being happy and free by disrupting the effort needed to achieve what you want.

True power is internal. It is the creative energy that turns your desires and ideas into reality. It is the concentration that allows you to overcome distractions and challenges to accomplish your goals. It is also the humility to drop the urge to fight or control life, the love and strength to hold back negative impulses, and the mastery over your conscious, unconscious, and subconscious mind. You reclaim it by disbelieving your sense of otherness trying to veil your perception with the idea that your obstacles are external, or that your value relies on how others judge or respond to you.

The ego dilutes your efforts with painful emotions, which is how it makes itself felt. For example, it may distort your creative power into the destructive energy of anger. If you act on it, your actions create impressions that will bring suffering. If you don't act on it, but you cannot find a positive way to channel this energy, then it goes inward, against yourself, disturbing the flow of prana and producing physical imbalances or depression. The ego actualizes your negative tendencies in your reality; you transform them as you grow emotionally, by letting go of what makes you feel safe simply because it is familiar. Outdated beliefs trigger resistance and hold you back, so you need to uncover the motivations and attachments behind them. (The Radical Honesty Process from Chapter Five can help you with this.)

At the level of ego consciousness, familiar situations and interactions, even if unpleasant, feel safer than the unknown. And yet, the future is always unknown; you uncover it only as your life-movie unfolds. It is the emotional energy of repetitive patterns that makes it seem less scary—unless, of course, you challenge your sense of otherness. You can walk toward the future seeking external validation, thus spinning in the perception of your wounded child archetype, or you can embrace whatever comes to you with the light of self-awareness and love.

In time, as you continue to dismiss the illusion of separation and *otherness*, your egoic sense of self will dissolve in the eternal Self like a stick that burns out after it has been used to stir up a fire. You may start by redirecting your mind inward to recognize how (and how often) you have disempowered yourself through your emotional codependency—that is, valuing yourself only *through* other people or identifying with their behaviors and the feelings they trigger in you. Here are some examples of how you may be doing this:

- You perceive others as more important, intelligent, creative, attractive, knowledgeable, interesting, successful, or spiritual than you, and you tend to diminish yourself in comparison.

- You have difficulty setting clear boundaries and feel guilty if you don't please other people or tend to their needs.

- You take emotional responsibility for your relationships and complain that the other person is not there for you.

- You let fears, doubts, stress, or a sense of obligation dictate your choices.

- You believe overextending yourself makes you a good person, yet you secretly resent not being appreciated for all you give.

- You focus on what is wrong or missing in your life, but you neglect expressing what you want, taking care of yourself, or doing what you enjoy.

- You belittle your talents, accomplishments, or experience, and crave external validation to feel worthy.

For an ordinary person, life is about social engagement and material success. For a true spiritual seeker, however, it is about finding inner peace through self-knowledge or devotion to something bigger than the ego-mind. Without self-awareness, though, what appears bigger may be a projection of the internal figures you have feared or idealized. Your sense of otherness blurs your discrimination with outdated illusions, which makes you vulnerable to manipulation and falling for false gurus, prophets, or cult leaders promising some type of salvation.

No religion, group, or person can liberate or save you from your own mental deception and the karma resulting from it. Once you comprehend that your life is a personalized movie—a dream within a dream—the fantasy of external salvation disappears. What is there to free yourself from but the virtual reality of your ego? It is quite the paradox! Nobody else can live or transform your life, because you are your life. You may learn from everyone and everything. You may honor the Divine in any form you choose. You may also have the privilege of encountering truly enlightened teachers or truly enlightening teachings. But only *you* can conquer your ego-mind by dissolving it in your Inner Self or surrendering it completely to God.

To reduce the codependency of *otherness* that keeps the ego active, it is essential to express yourself honestly, letting go of the self-images that enslave you to a wounded need for approval. You are here to express in action who you really are; this is what your body and mind are for. Use them as your tools while removing the mental, emotional, material, and spiritual greed of your ego to experience the inner peace of simply *being*. Turning it into a more permanent state requires three things: positive karma, a relentless effort to master the ego-mind, and Grace. Clearly, you also need these to accomplish anything.

Your life is an imaginary bubble within the cosmic dream of Consciousness. Nothing is really under your control or happens without Divine Will. Remember this to stay on track, unburdened by the idea of being the doer or *experiencer* of your reality through sensory perception, because this is also what turns you into the *sufferer*. Investigate the greedy nature of the ego with its endless desires. Observe it as it wants to be special or superior, craving more tools, more practices, more rituals, and more knowledge; although all these may be useful, blindly fostering desires to meet the needs of your ego prevents you from delving deeper within to find what you are really looking for. Watch it become spiritualized as you progress on your path as well.

Your mental patterns are woven with past impressions and unfulfilled desires. If you stop investing in them, they eventually go to sleep; but if you reinforce them with your emotional energy, they will continue distorting your perception, causing unpleasant situations that suck up your energy. It is like feeding a monster that demands increasing amounts of food as it gets bigger. By its very nature, the ego is addictive. When you take it for your identity, you strengthen the belief that you cannot *be* without your thoughts and identifications, which are just mental fluctuations carrying false ideas about yourself.

Once you start unraveling old patterns, the yearning for inner freedom increases. How long it takes to put them to sleep depends on how quickly you recognize and starve them of your energy. If, rather than blindly following your impulses, you observe and restrain them, you open up to new possibilities of experience. Any impulse loses momentum when you hold it back to gain clarity about the energy pushing you to follow it. If you intentionally anchor yourself in the present, you are able to watch your impulses and emotions come and go, like waves in the ocean.

However, anytime you take steps toward greater freedom, your sense of otherness will attempt to regain control with unconscious guilt and fear. It does this through your own perception, actualizing external opposition or demands to stall your process. If you believe your inner bully, appearing as people and events, you give it your power and let it deter you from pursuing your goals. If you recognize it for what it is, rather than taking things personally or focusing on others, your movie will spontaneously shift, and you can keep going.

I will explore this in more detail shortly, but for now it may be useful to imagine your ego as an octopus trying to direct your behavior with a variety of emotional "tentacles" triggering your negative patterns. This happens mostly through others, although it can also happen as internal chatter, which is your sense of otherness talking to your sense of self. Here are a few examples:

- Guilt/Shame: "This is your fault." "You should be ashamed." "What you are doing is wrong." "Look what you made me do." "You are selfish." "You are not supportive." "You don't care about me." "You don't care about my feelings." "How can you do this to me?" "You hate me."

- Fear: "What you want is impossible, too hard, too much." "You won't succeed." "You don't have what it takes." "You will be in trouble." "You will get hurt." "You will be sorry."

- Codependency: "I need you." "I cannot live/do this without you." "Why are you rejecting me?" "I am doing this just for you." "You should do this/that for me." "You don't need anyone but me." "We are soul mates."

- Control: "I am saying/doing this for your own good." "You need to do things my way." "You are not a good partner, friend, etc." "You cannot be trusted." "I know that's not how you feel." "You are too shy, sensitive, awkward, loud, intense, serious …" "You should be more mature, independent, creative, social, friendly, spiritual …"

- Aggression: "You are wrong, weak, stupid …" "You don't know what you are talking about." "You make me angry." "You are the worst." "I hate you." "You will pay for this."

- Passive aggression: "You are overreacting." "I don't know what you are talking about." "It is not my fault." "I cannot say anything to you." "You are so sensitive, angry, negative …" "You have changed." "I won't talk to you anymore."

- Opposition: "That's a bad idea." "You don't know what you are doing." "You should be doing … (what I want)." "You are making a mistake." "You don't really want to do that." "You don't have what it takes."

- Flattery/Manipulation: "You are so special, smart, gorgeous, spiritual …" "You are perfect for me." "There is something so unique about you." "You are the only one who really understands me." "We have something very special." "Can't you see how much I need you?"

Now, someone sincerely expressing their love for you is quite different from someone saying, "I love you" to manipulate you or cover up their controlling or abusive behavior. A good friend or partner shares their appreciation or concern without trying to exploit your wounded needs for their selfish agenda or to make themselves feel better, which is a reflection of internalized power dynamics. It can be confusing, so pay attention to any red flags, while cultivating and trusting your inner voice, to discern between fantasy and reality. Observe people's actual actions instead of blindly believing their words or justifying their behavior out of loyalty for something they did in the past.

Keep in mind that your sense of otherness uses these hooks to block your individuation and awareness of the truth. They will appear when you start stretching beyond familiar patterns to express yourself more freely or end toxic interactions, as well as when you take steps toward greater emotional and spiritual freedom. In other words, when you take more room in your life-movie. If the ego-octopus hooks you, you will feel compelled to justify or explain yourself, which means your wounded child archetype is taking over your perception.

If you are mindful enough not to get hooked by one of the emotional tentacles, another one is sure to follow, and then another. Watching your thoughts and impulses is critical to avoid reacting from a wounded place, spinning in outdated patterns you no longer want in your life. More often than not, what others say or do has nothing to do with you; they are reacting to their sense of otherness. You cannot control how they see you or how they act, but you can choose how to respond without identifying with their behavior. If you view difficult interactions as reflections of the distorted self-perception from your sense of otherness, you reclaim the power to transform your experience by managing your emotional energy. The key is shifting your awareness *from otherness to self*.

There are various aspects at play in the interaction with another person. There is their movie, which you can see if you are detached and objective enough to understand that person. Then, there is your movie, resulting from your past and present karma, as well as your mental patterns; it is therefore completely subjective. The intersection between those two movies, where any exchange of energy takes place, is where the sense of otherness is engaged. Yours colors your perception, and the other person's taints their viewpoint, since you can only live *your* movie, and they can only experience theirs. Now, if you have no control over their perception and choices, why would you let them determine how you feel about yourself? Whenever personal boundaries are fuzzy, it means that there is an excess sense of otherness upholding the usual power dynamics and emotional codependency of your ego.

In practical terms, the energy, space, and time that make up your life-movie are intertwined and respond to a common pattern, so how you manage them is mirrored in how other people value them in your life-movie as well. It is clear that you give your power away when others take up too much of your energy, time, or space, either physically or mentally. Since time is the most measurable guide, it is useful to keep track of it to assess how much you spend investing in yourself, how much goes to others, and how much you waste because of distractions, procrastination, or resistance. Allowing too much *otherness* in your movie is bound to create imbalance and conflicts.

Time is a fluid, subjective mental construct that stretches or shrinks according to your level of engagement. The value of your time is also relative to where you place yourself in relation to other people and where you direct your attention. If you dwell on past, disagreeable situations, you let those impressions rob you of the present moment. By contrast, if you are fully anchored in yourself, in the present, you align with the infinite nature of Divine Consciousness, the eternal *here and now* that is the backdrop of all fluctuations of energy. Events appear to follow a timeline, but you can only experience each moment here and now, as your life unfolds, before it turns into a memory.

Neither the past nor the future exists; it is the ego-mind that jumps back and forth to disconnect you from the present. Only the present is real, and it is your place of power. When you are not centered, anchored in the moment, it is easy to be driven by past, wounded needs—such as the need to be liked, needed, or useful—and give away too much of your energy-time-space. Those around you will respond with matching patterns of *otherness* to meet yours. These are unconscious points of resonance that bring you together, in addition to the conscious ones, like similar interests or beliefs.

A personal relationship becomes imbalanced when you give more energy-time-space than your partner. If you take emotional responsibility for the relationship, they don't need to put in any effort, or they will demand more attention and control. You may be reproducing old, dysfunctional dynamics that can quickly turn into power struggles. If love gets too distorted with unresolved emotions and expectations, rather than removing the sense of separation, it may bring an increasing disconnection from one another. However, your life is your movie, so it is ultimately about *you*, both as a projection of your ego and as the road map you need to navigate to mature emotionally and spiritually.

Your soul's inherent drive for individuation is the inner pull toward Oneness. Since the ego creates and exists only in duality, it seeks a false oneness in the apparent union with another ego—that is, another appearance of itself. Through this delusion, it makes you think you are incomplete, on some level, without your "other half." In reality, what makes you long for someone else is your desire for pleasure, validation, and love. The fleeting ecstasy of sensual passion, when the ego momentarily disappears, offers a brief glimpse into your blissful essence, but it quickly gives way to an egoic attachment that distorts love with the idea that it must be expressed as sensory gratification.

Life is a dream of multiplicity sustained by the instinctual attraction between living beings. But you don't need another person to complete you, for you are Divine Consciousness. You are limitless and eternal. It is your identification with the body and mind that alienates you from the totality you are. Your ego chases pleasure to hide the suffering it inherently causes through attraction, aversion, and fear. A happy person does not look for happiness, only an unhappy person does. And yet, happiness is what you are—the eternal Self abiding in your heart. You are love seeking love and falling in love with love while believing it is outside of you.

Even if oneness is not possible in the duality of *otherness*, you can certainly transform your interactions into *togetherness* by removing the self-centered expectations of your ego blocking love. This occurs naturally when you nurture your sense of self and engage with other people from this level of awareness. Otherwise, the ego-mind, which is the same in you and others, will keep seeking validation and gratification to protect its virtual existence while distorting your experience.

Think about it. You internalized your parental figures to reactivate the impressions and tendencies you came to resolve. Your mate also internalized their parental figures as their sense of otherness. Since you appear separate to each other, when you get together, you are connecting at this level of perception. There is a subtle, unconscious exchange going on, in spite of what either one of you consciously wants. You are not just interacting with the person you each see; you are also engaging with the unconscious figures and dynamics each of you carries within, through matching mental and emotional impressions, as well as shared karma and soul memories.

This intensifies if you get married, because your *emotional* tendencies toward partnership (or commitment) were reflected by your parents, and now your unconscious beliefs compel you to reproduce. It becomes even more obvious if you have children, when those internal voices and figures push familiar reactions, even if you are making a conscious effort not to behave like your parents. As a dynamic aspect of ego, your sense of otherness is an elusive blend of people, voices, emotions, and beliefs that overlap, so it is not easy to recognize how certain patterns reinforce each other, because your ego disguises them. Someone once told me, "I was so determined not to marry a man like my father that I didn't notice I was marrying one like my mother!"

You are most likely to relate to a person who shares various aspects with your father, your mother, your siblings, and any other important figures from childhood, because you carry similar or complementary seeds of perception. Other people will invariably reflect your sense of otherness; and the closer the relationship, the more intense the reflection. For this reason, being at peace with your parents is essential to be at peace with your past and the world. It does not mean you have to please them or condone abusive behaviors, but you need to see and accept them for who they are or were, rather than holding on to illusions of who you think they should have been. Appreciate that they served as vehicles for you to continue your human adventure. In this egoic world, it is very hard to be a child, but it is also very hard to be a parent.

You need to see them clearly to know yourself. A good exercise to recognize the internal figures and voices in your sense of otherness is writing about each of your parents from a neutral perspective, as if you were a journalist. Explore everything you know about them as individuals, not just as parents, removing any judgments or expectations they failed to meet. Write about their story, dreams, aspirations, and unresolved issues. Tune in to their perception of life, of themselves, and of others, as well as their reactions when faced with challenges or distress. Then try to recognize some of those aspects in your own attitudes, actions, and beliefs about yourself and others, and how they get reflected in your life-movie.

You know your parents better than you think, even if you don't have much information or remember everything, because you have been paying close attention to them all your life, observing and often resonating with their hidden tendencies. They probably haven't changed much from when you were a child anyway, and some of their (and your) patterns have been reinforced for generations. Seeing these authority figures can help you see yourself more clearly as well, by recognizing the ideas you have in common that now hamper your process of individuation and your relationships.

Obviously, you are not your parents; you have a unique path and purpose. Like everyone else, they are appearances of Consciousness helping you become conscious of yourself. However, the seeds of perception you have shared with them are significant and get energized through your sense of otherness when you interact with the world. If you don't connect the dots between those figures, your past, and your ego-mind, you simply drag to your relationships similar dysfunctional dynamics to those of childhood, as well as unresolved issues with your family and previous partners.

Although some carry more energy and are more intense or important than others, all relationships are karmic; romantic relationships are no exception. There is an energetic resonance that draws two people to each other. When you fall in love, a few things are taking place: a deep yearning for your true nature, which is love; shared soul memories and causal seeds from past experiences; an instinctual, sensual attraction veiling the rational mind with the desire for pleasure; and your sense of otherness activating past impressions and illusions from wounded needs in search of resolution.

As the relationship develops, the pleasure and excitement of the initial attraction give way to familiar habits of perception, thus bringing your sense of otherness to the forefront. You expect your partner to be an idealized version of you, to meet your unfulfilled needs and illusions; and your mate expects the same of you. Since neither of you can be anything other than yourselves, these hidden expectations create conflicts.

You may start seeing annoying things about the other person that you couldn't see before, or your interactions become repetitive. But now you are attached, and if they don't express love or support the way your wounded child archetype needs it, you feel hurt and confused. Some of the enjoyable aspects that made that person seem special can easily turn into points of disconnection that start building resentment. Without self-awareness and emotional maturity on both ends, you can only relate at the level of ego—through your sense of otherness—which may create a mismatch between your individual views and expressions of love.

You see your partner as the source of your disappointment and grief. If you are completely honest, however, you can recognize that your dissatisfaction and painful feelings preceded this and other relationships. The ego-mind keeps spinning in old patterns, so you blame your mate for what you haven't healed in yourself. It is like carrying a little package of unresolved issues you readily project onto whoever triggers them. The emotions are yours, as well as the beliefs behind them; the other person is simply reflecting your sense of otherness, just like you are a mirror for theirs.

For this reason, arguments tend to revolve around repetitive, familiar issues. Even if you work things out and come to an agreement, the ego-mind will continue to bring them up over and over, until you resolve them in yourself. Of course, if you just fixate on others, you cannot see any of this clearly. Trying to control or convince someone to change in order to meet your needs is making them responsible for your emotions, which is a reflection of past, family interactions. You're really giving your power to the inner bully that sabotages your relationship—by distorting love—rather than taking responsibility for your own outdated perception.

Since it hampers your individuation with the sense that *you should be someone other than who you are, doing something other than what you are doing (or want to do)*, you perceive other people through this lens, unconsciously refusing to accept who they are as well. Everyone is experiencing their life-movie through their sense of otherness. Nobody can read your mind or see things exactly like you, because they are not you. If you step back to acknowledge that you are engaging through the coloring of your ego, you will be able to see what your movie is really showing you about yourself and let go of the false ideas that make you unhappy. Self-awareness can shift old dynamics and transform your experience. The key is remembering that *your life is your movie*, and that real change can only happen from within you.

Every exchange of energy is an opportunity to uncover your negative tendencies and beliefs, but only if you turn inward instead of fixating on other people. When you embrace life as a soul-guided journey of self-discovery, you accept the world as it is and people as they are, dismissing what you think they *should* be. By purifying your mind of this self-centeredness, which is an essential quality of your ego, you naturally take a more neutral stance from which love is not always polluted by drama or pain. Reducing the excess *otherness* in your perception lets you navigate life more peacefully, without so much resistance.

While growing up, other people's needs seemed more important than yours, so you learned to perceive yourself in relation to them. Now, seeking a deeper connection to yourself invariably triggers unconscious forms of guilt and fear. For instance, you may start new projects without bringing them to fruition. You may expect instant gratification and give up when you face obstacles. You may question your decisions out of fear of judgment or opposition. You may be distracted from your goals when others need something from you, or you disrupt your process with doubts and anxiety.

The problem is not that you want to be of service to others; the issue is doing it impulsively, taking on fixed, familiar roles to feel safe or gain validation. It is doing things with the hidden self-interest to prove that you are good, useful, responsible, or spiritual in order to justify your existence. This secretly feeds your ego by trying to compensate for an ingrained sense of deficiency or insufficiency it inherently creates. That being said, when you act from a spirit of true selfless service, putting others before you with no ulterior motive or expectations of any kind, or at least consciously dismissing them as they arise, you cultivate positive tendencies and balance out old karmic debts.

Your life-movie will always show you where you are at, both in terms of your accomplishments as well as the internal patterns that cause you pain. By unraveling them, you clear the outdated coloring that taints your experiences. Furthermore, by developing the discipline to watch your life as a movie, you come to recognize that *you are not your mind or your body*, or their energy fluctuations. You are the one who observes them. You have the power not to believe or follow any of your thoughts, impulses, or desires. If, instead of identifying with them, you view your reality as a creation and reflection of your ego, you transform it by reclaiming the control of your perception.

This requires ongoing mindfulness, since the natural direction of ego is outward. Cultivate the habit of inquiring:

"Where is my attention?"

"Is it on others?" – It is, if you are focused outward, either fixating on, judging, envying, criticizing, psychoanalyzing, or identifying with other people to protect your self-images instead of observing yourself.

"Is it on me, but in relation to others?" – It is, if you feel insecure or self-conscious because you perceive yourself through other people's behavior, either comparing yourself to them, feeling judged, or fearing their judgment, while also seeking validation rather than valuing yourself for who you are.

"Or is it anchored in myself?" – It is, when you are centered and fully present, while also remaining detached, therefore able to embrace your experience as it is.

Your energy follows your attention, so it is easy to disconnect from yourself when your focus is on others or on yourself in relation to others. To remain centered, self-aware, and at ease while you engage with the world, you need a solid anchor to restrain the ego-mind from drawing you outward. You can develop it by integrating creative and spiritual practices that leave imprints of inwardness and neutrality.

An ongoing project helps you develop the concentration and single-mindedness you need to meditate and to stay centered when you deal with different people and situations. If done in solitude and silence, your endeavor can bring clarity about yourself, as you watch the thoughts and feelings arising in your mental field. In addition, it nurtures your imagination, intuition, discernment, and discipline.

If used as an introspective practice, immersing yourself in activities like writing, playing music, drawing, painting, dancing, ceramics, or photography provides a pause from the usual fixation on *otherness*, therefore nurturing your sense of self and making it easier for you to direct your attention as needed. It also connects you to the flow of creative and healing energy within you—the Feminine principle of Consciousness. But it has to be a regular, solitary activity for you to notice the effects, and it must be done for its own sake, with no attachment, expectations, or agendas. The moment these appear is a sign that your ego is trying to control your experience. Don't do it for validation or with the idea of being productive either; not everything in life has to be functional or profitable.

It is a time to invite and let your little orphans play! The main purpose is your self-expression while also training your mind to turn *from otherness to self*. Think of it as your sense of self taking more room in your movie by dropping the need for external input or approval. If you are a creative professional, then try something different than what you do for work or business, and do it only for its own sake. The aim is being fully present in what you are doing.

Watch your thoughts and feelings through the process, and use the final result to ponder, "What does this reflect about me?" When you are completely focused, you create an opening for insight and wisdom to emerge. Don't let the ego-mind hijack it. Remain aware without indulging in intellectual or logical analysis. Being anchored in yourself takes time and effort, but you can strengthen your process by approaching all other activities in a similar manner, with increasing mindfulness and focus. Inquire regularly, *"Where is my attention? Is it on others, is it on myself in relation to others, or is it anchored in me?"* Then bring it back to your heart—the center of your experience.

In addition, daily meditation is essential. You may start by sitting for an increasing period, but keep in mind that the real goal is to be able to maintain a meditative state throughout the day: a state of *non-action* or *no*-mind—that is, without ego. A daily discipline trains the mind to turn inward, weakening its natural tendency to jump from past to future; from thoughts to feelings to desires; from imaginations to rational concepts; and everything in between. Since the breath controls the mind, I am offering a simple meditation where the focal point is the breath to help you remain focused.

Meditation creates a space where the usual preoccupations fade away, thus allowing a flow of *sattvic* energy to take over. It is an opening for Consciousness to loosen old patterns and energy knots by dissolving the ego-mind. Although it benefits you on physical, emotional, and creative levels, the real goal of meditation is achieving superconscious states where there is no sense of experience for the ego to claim—only Pure Awareness. These states of *no-thing-ness* leave imprints that effect a gradual yet profound transformation of your psyche.

Practice is crucial. Start with the following meditation for at least twenty to thirty minutes every day, which will prepare you for a deeper practice in the last chapter of the book. Obviously, your ego-mind will resist it, pulling you away from it with distractions and discomforts. Be determined to persevere, or the ego will continue to control your behavior, keeping you trapped in the past and the painful delusion of duality. If you are committed to transforming your life-movie from within—by directing your awareness *from otherness to self*—your reality will shift effortlessly and you will experience greater peace and freedom.

***

Anchoring in the Consciousness "I Am"

This meditation promotes inwardness by redirecting the mind. At first, you may create a sacred atmosphere to practice. However, the goal is to turn it into an ongoing mental discipline you maintain no matter where you are, with your eyes open. A daily practice is meant to train the mind, but it should lead to a continuous state of simply *being*.

Choose a spot where you will not be interrupted. Sit with your spine straight and relaxed, gently resting your hands on your lap. Close your eyes and become aware of any noises, sensations, feelings, and thoughts. Don't fixate on them, just observe. You may briefly acknowledge them in a neutral, objective manner. For instance, "Tension ... thoughts ... noise ... pain ... memories ... irritation ..." Take a deep, long breath to leave them all out there, and focus your attention on your breathing. Observe the air moving in and out of your nose. Don't try to direct your breathing; keep it natural and just watch.

Start following each inhalation and exhalation alternating the mantras *Soham* and *Hamsa* you learned at the end of Chapter Two. At a subtle level, these are the sounds of the inner breath of the Self or Pure Awareness. Think *So* as you inhale and *Ham* as you exhale, then think *Ham* as you inhale and *Sa* as you exhale. You don't have to imagine or visualize anything, simply focus on the sounds as the breath goes in and out: *So ... Ham ... Ham ... Sa ... So ... Ham ... Ham ... Sa ...*

Once your mind is quieter, direct your attention further inward, to your heart, and anchor your breathing here by turning *Soham* into "I am." Do not think of the breath going in and out anymore, but rather going "in and in" as you focus on your heart; your breathing will become subtler as you concentrate on "I am," excluding anything that is not "I am." This is the core of your existence, of all your experiences, and there is nothing here except the feeling "I am." Relax into it by refusing any other thoughts. Don't be concerned with visions, intuitions, messages, or sensations, which are mere distractions. Breathe into your heart and remain in the consciousness "I am." Whenever you catch yourself thinking, immediately inquire:

"Who is having these thoughts?"
and
"Who is aware of these thoughts?"

Focus on the awareness rather than the mental activity to delve further within, as you bring your attention back to your heart with, "I am." This is your anchor; it should exclude everything else. Stay here by rejecting other, uninvited thoughts trying to pull you away from it. Whenever they arise, bring yourself back to your center by asking again, *"Who is aware of these thoughts?"* Do this as many times as needed to anchor in the "I am." If you persevere, your consciousness will gradually dissolve into Stillness. It takes time and persistence, so don't get discouraged if it seems like a struggle at first; just keep at it. Although the ego-mind will resist, it has to surrender at some point.

When you are coming out of meditation, gently open your eyes and try to maintain this state of inwardness while you tend to your activities, keeping some of your attention on your heart, in the consciousness "I am." If you do this, you will not be as reactive or give your power away to the excessive *otherness* you usually allow in your life-movie. Anchor yourself in your heart with "I am" whenever you encounter a stressful situation, to deal with it in a detached, centered manner.

The mind is a revolving factory of thoughts. Its activity diminishes when you stop following it blindly to regain the power to direct it at will. Practice this at least twenty to thirty minutes every day, and continue integrating it into your daily life by keeping some of your attention anchored in your heart with the feeling "I am." If you have difficulty concentrating, first do the *Soham-Hamsa* Pranayama from Chapter Two.

CHAPTER EIGHT

Healing the Past Through the Present

Indeed the whole world is yours, of your Self, your very own – but you perceive it as separate, just as you see "others." To know it to be your own gives happiness, but the notion that it is apart from you causes misery.

—Anandamayi Ma

An old Taoist man suddenly fell ill. Within a week, his state had become quite grave, so his worried sons called in three physicians. The first doctor examined him and gave his opinion saying that, even though the sickness was serious, it could be treated. After hearing this, the old man called him a charlatan and ordered his sons to get rid of him.

Then the second physician came forward, proclaiming that the causes leading to his illness were of slow, gradual growth, making it incurable. The father told him he was a good doctor and asked his sons to feed him before sending him away.

Lastly, the third medic announced that his illness was attributable neither to God nor to man, nor to the agency of spirits; that it was already preordained in the mind of Providence at birth, and no herbs or drugs could be of any use to him. Hearing these observations, the old Taoist exclaimed, "You are indeed a physician from Heaven!" Then he instructed his children to give him many presents before seeing him out. Soon after, his illness disappeared on its own.

When we identify with the physical body, which is what keeps us trapped in ego consciousness, suffering weaves the fabric of our life; such is the drama of the human condition. You experience the world of polarities through the sensory perception that sets in motion your actions and reactions, but it also constricts the eternal nature of your soul. You seek bodily pleasures in an attempt to escape the painful restriction of being in a human body, but it is your very search that causes you distress; it expresses an innate yearning that is impossible to satisfy with anything external.

You look for happiness outside of yourself, getting attached to impermanent things that eventually bring about suffering, and you keep trying to free yourself from it. This is a vicious circle that revolves through your patterns of perception. Your reality is a modification of Consciousness, a mirage actualizing the content of your causal body in your mental field, which is basically a collection of impressions, tendencies, and karma from previous experiences projected as your individual life-movie. If you want to transform it, you need to heal the past you have identified with, which means liberating yourself from it, leaving it behind so that it no longer distorts or disconnects you from the present.

At the level of ego consciousness, you expect your desires to be fulfilled, and you become discouraged or resentful if things don't go the way you want. But when you fight or resist life, you reinforce the egoic need to control it which produces the anger, discontentment, and destructive actions that disconnect you from yourself. By contrast, accepting *what is as it is*, as it plays out, changes the inertial direction of old tendencies, to bring new possibilities of experience. These shifts cannot happen without self-knowledge. You have to see how your sense of otherness traps you emotionally in the past to be able to release the outdated ideas that make you unhappy.

But once you understand how predictable the ego-mind is, you can take advantage of its revolving quality to break free from old, toxic dynamics as you grow out of the emotional codependency that reinforces your sense of otherness. After all, it is made of unresolved emotions and false beliefs about yourself. Rather than blaming other people for your afflictions, you must remain attentive to your inner bully trying to punish you whenever you don't comply with its demands or expectations.

This happens through your self-perception, so it can take many forms, such as pressure or stress, anxiety, anger, depression, loneliness, shame, addictions, hopelessness, or physical ailments, as well as unconscious actions that sabotage your process of individuation—in a nutshell, anything that diminishes your sense of self. In this cosmic play of Consciousness, your greatest power is self-awareness, because it leads to Self-realization. It transmutes ignorance into light and egoism into love, gradually revealing the truth that you are the Pure Awareness where everything unfolds. You have everything you need to be free, because you are already free; it is the false ideas from which you are used to experiencing your life that veil this truth.

Your life-movie is like a mirror showing you where you are at, as well as what you need to release to be at peace with yourself and the world. If you accept that what shows up in it is your own projection appearing as something separate—your *otherness*—you can take full spiritual responsibility for your reality and heal the past that it is reflecting back at you. Instead of fixating on other people, you explore your perception to understand what may be distorting your experience, and how. You drop the usual victim-blame and power games that keep the ego in control, to uncover the source of your thoughts, feelings, and motivations.

Everything in your reality is a symbolic expression of your subconscious content. You just have to discern it with a more intuitive approach to find connections between your outer and inner worlds. For instance, you can explore the symbolism of changes in your immediate environment or of physical symptoms and injuries by observing how they make you *feel* and what they prevent you from doing. A simple example would be your car breaking down or you having muscle or joint pain, which may be symbolic expressions of your resistance to move forward. By examining what any event means to *you* and how it makes *you* feel (rather than just a general symbolism), you redirect your attention inward to uncover its source.

You navigate your life-movie as it unfolds within the cosmic dream of the Self. The first step toward emotional and spiritual freedom is accepting that you, your mind, your life, and the people in it are not separate. They are individualized appearances of Consciousness through which you experience and know yourself, which is the true purpose of your journey and the way to transcend your human condition. As you investigate the repeating patterns in your interactions with others, you starve them of your energy and gradually put them to sleep.

Your hurdles in life are not just external issues resulting from conditioning or "programming," as if you were a blank slate or a robot; they are deeply ingrained, predominant tendencies of self-perception weaving painful experiences. These mental patterns have been coming around and will continue to do so until they run out of energy. When you start exploring them, they will reappear, disguised in different ways, thanks to the shape-shifting quality of your ego. But if you keep at it, without identifying with the emotions they bring up, they will take longer to return and hold less energy when they do, which means they will be less and less triggering. However, they are persistent; they may take subtler forms or stop for a while, only to cycle back down the road, unexpectedly. I have seen certain dynamics manifest again after fading for twenty or thirty years, although usually with very little energy.

Since the ego-mind is not only revolving but also mobile and deceptive, you must observe your patterns over and over until they become so predictable you can see them clearly without having to engage with them. Never underestimate the relentless nature of your ego; its mission is to take over your true Self by hindering self-awareness. Thinking that you have resolved an issue by rationalizing, processing, or psychoanalyzing it is an illusion. Until they roast in steady superconscious states or pure devotion, your causal seeds remain latent when they are not active. Their strength diminishes as your awareness increases, but they always hold the potential to bloom if given a fertile terrain.

Processing may be important to gain clarity about yourself and the situations you are in, but it is just one aspect of your healing. Also, be careful not to overanalyze things, which is a form of resistance that prevents you from letting go or from taking action. Dwelling on what you already understand is another way the ego-mind keeps you spinning in place. Try to go deeper, peeling layer after layer of distorted ideas and beliefs to remove negative seeds of perception.

Spirituality is self-knowledge. Without knowing your ego-mind, you cannot touch the Inner Self, because the ego keeps you trapped in a sensory perception and the delusion of duality or *otherness*. Knowing yourself means recognizing what you *believe* yourself to be, which is what prevents you from simply *being* who and what you truly are. All impulses, desires, thoughts, memories, and beliefs come and go. You can watch them come and go precisely because they are not you. When you stop identifying with them, they lose momentum and fade away.

Perceiving your life as a mental projection of the past offers a doorway into your psyche. Once you embrace it as a journey of self-discovery, you stop seeing challenges as problems you are supposed to fix to be happy, and instead appreciate them as opportunities to uncover what has been hidden from you. Your movie unfolds like a karmic dream within a dream, with events that shape the road map you are meant to navigate: the situations you have to endure, the lessons you must learn, and the aspects you have cultivated, as well as those that remain unresolved. Since the real purpose of it all is to reclaim your true Self, only what you discover and experience on your own, through self-awareness, can be of lasting use to you.

If you relinquish the need to control anything, inner clarity and guidance will emerge spontaneously. If you watch yourself honestly in your day-to-day activities and interactions, without judging or resisting, you engage with your life-movie from within to make conscious choices toward greater freedom. This is not freedom from or in relation to *others*; it is freedom from your ego-mind, which is real, lasting freedom. It demands nurturing positive seeds of perception while starving the ones that recreate situations causing you pain. But you cannot just *think*

Healing the Past Through the Present

your way out of an unpleasant reality by rationalizing or suppressing your emotions; you need to be aware of the underlying patterns weaving your experience, or they will keep repeating time and again, blocking the authentic expression of your soul.

To implement the Swan Method and start effecting change in your life-movie, it is important to comprehend three fundamental aspects:

1. *Your current reality is a projection of the past.* All life events result from past karma, and your perception of them is also invariably colored with the emotional energy of past impressions and desires.

2. *The past no longer exists.* You are who you are now. To be fully present, you must stop identifying with the outdated beliefs about yourself reflected in your reality by investigating and dissolving them.

3. *You cannot control the current projection.* You can only shift your perception from here on out, because you cannot change the past. But every experience is exactly what you need, moment to moment, to recognize your predominant negative patterns of perception and behavior.

Your experience of the present is tainted by the past because the ego-mind is made of past impressions. You may notice that your environment echoes the past as well. That is, you perceive and surround yourself with memories. Besides your mental-emotional fluctuations, some may be displayed as photographs or souvenirs while others may be more emotional, like paintings, diplomas, awards, gifts, borrowed things, and objects that remind you of certain people and events. Subtler soul memories are revealed by the cultures, traditions, styles, symbols, preferences, and activities to which you are drawn, as well as your innate talents resulting from previous efforts.

Not only do you identify with your stories and would feel lost without them. On a deeper level, you also get a sense of direction and purpose from the impressions and desires you unconsciously carry and project. They appear as your world and pull you outward to experience yourself in different situations. You are like a spider living in a complex mental web you have built with your thoughts and desires. You learn to make better choices from the various events occurring on this web, gradually refining the ego-mind through both evolution (or experience) and involution (or introspection), until it becomes so thin through your discrimination that it dissolves in Consciousness.

Ultimately, you are who you are *now*—not who you have been before, who you would like to become, or who you think you should be. All situations on your path, whether pleasant or painful, spiritual or mundane, have led you right here. Being fully present means embodying the eternal presence of the Inner Self you are—your essential *I-am-ness*—even if momentarily. This is your center, your place of power, where the divisions and fluctuations of the mind disappear.

No matter how many changes you have gone through and how many more you may undergo, this *I-am-ness* is the one constant on your journey that links you to the timelessness and totality of your true Self. Although fluid, only the present is real; it is the flow of life itself, continuously changing and expanding. You cannot go back in time to change things, but you can transform your perception from where you are by shedding light onto the past reflected in your life-movie. Clearly, you have to stop seeing life as something external and separate from you; otherwise, you will miss the opportunities to see the patterns and tendencies from which it originates, and these will just continue revolving and galvanizing painful beliefs about yourself.

If you remember that your reality is a personal movie reflecting your egoic sense of otherness, you free yourself from an outdated self-perception and the false ideas that sustain the delusion of duality. The ego-mind will make this very fuzzy, however, drawing your attention outward by fixating on other people to deter you from looking within. The external world arises from and is made of ego. It shows you where you are in terms of desires, goals, and accomplishments, as well as any unresolved issues that taint your experience of reality. You cannot avoid or pretend that an unpleasant situation isn't there; denial is the opposite of awareness, and awareness is the force that transforms your life-movie. You must tend to it, but you can engage with it as a humble vehicle of Consciousness, rather than the doer, without reacting to or identifying with it.

Try to find the path of least resistance toward the solution or change the situation requires; if you see what it is really pointing out in your perception, it will shift spontaneously. The key is remembering that it is *your movie*, and the choices you make will affect how you experience it from here on out. It all happens from within you, from the eternal Self you are and everything else is as well. If you don't see your mental-emotional patterns, you will keep investing in painful dynamics that will continue revolving until you remove what fuels them. For instance, if you tend to argue or fight about something but cannot see your wounded need to fight, control, or be right, then your movie will reflect this negative tendency again and again through new situations giving you plenty of reasons to argue or fight.

You must remain centered and detached to observe what is going on, investing about ten percent of your emotional energy and time toward a solution or agreement, and keeping the other ninety percent for what connects you to you *now*—your self-discovery, projects, and goals. This way, you weaken old negative patterns and impulses while opening up to new possibilities. Of course, it is a process, so you may start with a different percentage ratio. Keep in mind the aim is to get to a point where you invest most of your energy in what keeps you anchored in yourself and less in your sense of otherness, which activates fears or illusions about the future because it represents the past with which you are familiar. Negative feelings triggered by a current situation are merely echoing unresolved emotions that prevent you from being present—anchored in yourself.

It is, again, a matter of redirecting your attention *from otherness to self*: going from what appears external to the exploration of what it is pointing at *in yourself*. If you are mainly focused outward, you experience life through your sense of otherness, driven by the unconscious needs of your wounded child archetype. When you are too invested in what others are doing or saying, you are not anchored in yourself. You have to mentally step back to observe and understand what any situation is really about—in you. This gives you a stronger standpoint and greater clarity of purpose as you participate in it.

Just like the external world disappears when you are asleep, if you direct your attention inward, your ego consciousness gradually dissolves, because you are less invested in your identifications. This means that the inherent, ego-based sense of dissatisfaction and insufficiency pushing you to seek validation also fades away. Self-awareness is love, and love heals your distorted perception of reality by removing the ignorance and egoism that keeps painful patterns in place. Moving forward, focus on discovering the main three things your life-movie is always showing you to help you grow: what you need to let go of, what you need to nurture, and what you need to develop—in yourself. An effective approach to gain insight into these aspects is inquiring, every step of the way:

"Why is this in my movie?"
and
"What is it pointing out in me?"

This should be an ongoing exploration. Your life is like a mirror that reflects how you perceive yourself *through* others. Since everyone experiences life colored by their perception and sense of otherness, and your interactions happen in the mental space where your movie and their movie intersect, pay attention to what that space is showing you by the way it makes you *feel* about yourself—not about others. If you start judging or blaming them for your negative emotions, you are simply identifying with their behavior, which has nothing to do with you, except on a subconscious level of resonance that creates the interaction. In the play of Consciousness, we reflect each other to become conscious of our perception.

You are responsible for yours, and everyone else is responsible for theirs. The most important aspect is to remember that your life mirrors your unconscious beliefs about yourself because, again, it is *your movie*. The ego-mind works the same way in everyone; it divides, judges, and finds fault to be in control. But how life unfolds is nobody's fault; it is a collective of experiences in the field of Consciousness from which we all learn and grow, albeit at an individual pace. Some people are where you have been, and you will be where others may be now. Your job is to discern what your life-movie reflects to you about yourself while interacting with others from a centered place of greater awareness.

Only when you start seeing yourself clearly, you can see other people more clearly as well, because removing false identifications allows a deeper understanding to emerge. By living your life from within, watching it as a fictional movie, you dismiss outdated impressions and illusions. The focus is on you, but not to judge yourself with the idea that you should be perfect or already know what you are in the process of learning. The main purpose is to become aware of what you need to release, nurture, and develop to break free from the deceptions of your ego-mind keeping you stuck in the past.

If an unpleasant situation arises, step back and observe how you feel. What negative emotions are being triggered? Be careful not to rationalize, judge, or justify them, which is what the ego will prompt you to do. Simply acknowledge your feelings without attachment or resistance. To feel your feelings, your mind has to turn inward; if you don't identify, you can recognize them as fluctuations of past emotional energy coloring your perception. They don't define you unless you act upon or hold on to them; they are simply pointing out what you need to see in yourself.

You uncover distorted patterns and beliefs through painful emotions because they reflect a perception tainted with wrong or outdated ideas about yourself, about others, about life. The fact that you can observe them proves that you are not your feelings, but you have to detach to be able to observe them. If you immediately become your feelings, you give all control to your sense of otherness. Instead, hold the impulse to react, demand, or prove anything, and remember to ask yourself:

> *"What am I so attached to?"*
> and
> *"What am I so afraid of?"*

The answers will relate to the self-images you have built to protect your ego. Once your attachments and fears come to light, you can drop them to find a freer, more creative way to express yourself without knee-jerk reactions that promote or keep negative dynamics in place. If you restrain your impulses, the emotional energy pushing you to follow them can come to your awareness. This gives you the opportunity to respond to the situation more objectively, rather than taking things personally, which is the self-centeredness of your ego, always expecting validation and gratification.

Once you are anchored in a more neutral place, you can find the path of least resistance to tend to your life-movie without investing more emotional energy than is needed. If you have a genuine desire to transform karmic dynamics, as well as the negative tendencies that reproduce them, the end result will be twofold: you will gain emotional maturity by growing out of the wounded child archetype (your past); and you will make more room for Divine Consciousness (love) to modify your life-movie from within.

Oftentimes, all it takes is listening to the other person with detachment and openness, rather than identifying with their reactions and feeling pressured to defend yourself or prove something. It is a matter of giving less room to your sense of otherness attempting to control your experience, with the understanding that nothing in your life is really separate from you. Being able to manage the energy of your life-movie from within is very empowering. Your usual fears start fading away, and if you get out of your way with the intention to see your reflection clearly, the movie shifts spontaneously without you needing to control or convince anyone of anything.

However, at the level of your ego consciousness, stepping back and surrendering to *what is*, by dropping the need to be right or find validation through others, turns you into you a "loser." Your inner bully may spin the issue in your head for days, months, or years, making you feel you should have fought more or gotten even in some way. This is a trick to keep you in the past, because all you are really losing is the very ego that creates your difficulties and suffering. The choice is yours every step of the way: you either reinforce old, negative patterns of perception or you make room for greater awareness and love to remove egoic power dynamics that disturb your inner peace.

Now, if you think such change isn't possible because the other person isn't going to cooperate and will react in the usual manner, it means you are trying to hide behind them to avoid taking full spiritual responsibility for your own movie. You have no control over anyone else's choices or behavior, but change can and will happen when you transform your perception by letting go of familiar yet outdated roles, attitudes, and ideas. Again, this is your mental movie, and nothing in it is separate from you!

Shifts will occur naturally through your effort to drop a distorted self-perception, which will affect how you perceive others and the world as well.

Main Guidelines

I will now provide step-by-step instructions for the Swan Method to heal the past and transform your life. To master it, it is important to maintain the two fundamental practices I have previously mentioned:

1. An ongoing creative activity or project to anchor yourself in the present, develop concentration, and nurture your self-expression. You should do this in addition to any other pursuits requiring complete focus.

2. A daily practice of Anchoring in the Consciousness "I am" (from the previous chapter) to cultivate stillness and sense withdrawal. Incorporate it in your everyday life as much as possible, and expand it, whenever you are ready, into the self-inquiry process you will learn in Chapter Nine (Living in Pure Awareness).

Be disciplined and consistent with your practices and implementing this Method. It may take some time to fully understand and integrate it, but if you persevere, your reward will be greater inner freedom. The basic foundation is observing your life with detachment and self-awareness, as a movie reflecting the content of your subconscious, while accepting everything as it unfolds. Act and participate, but *without reacting* to anything out of fear or negative tendencies. Instead, watch your mental activity to uncover your self-perception and how it has been tainted with a false sense of deficiency and vulnerability that is contrary to your divine nature.

Again, the main purpose is to redirect your awareness from *otherness* to self, to investigate the unconscious energy that keeps you emotionally in the past. I have italicized key elements and questions you should be constantly asking yourself. To take you through the steps of the process, I am focusing on situations that trigger negative emotions, but you should try to apply the Swan Method all the time by observing your thoughts and emotional states, as well as your environment, conversations, and experiences, to get to know yourself. You may feel more inclined to explore patterns of perception that show in dramatic, disruptive ways, but try to pay attention to subtle aspects, such as attitudes or beliefs that seem small yet reinforce painful ones—that is, how you view, discourage, or deflate yourself when you are alone.

- As you go through your life, make it a habit to inquire, *"Where is my attention?" Is it on others*, because I am fixating on other people? *Is it on me in relation to others*, because I am self-conscious, afraid to be judged, or insecure and seeking validation? *Or is it anchored in myself*, as I remain fully present and self-aware?" If it is not grounded in you, take a deep breath and regain your center in the consciousness "I am" to approach any situation with greater detachment.

- If you encounter a sudden difficulty, a challenging interaction, or any type of opposition that triggers negative emotions, remember that your external reality is a projection of the past reflecting your sense of otherness. This is essential to avoid reacting impulsively or losing yourself in your movie. Judging and fixating on others is a protective mechanism of the ego to prevent you from looking at yourself.

- Bring your attention to your heart and check in: *"How do I feel about this?"* Keep your awareness on your feelings and be honest; don't push, rationalize, or identify with them. Accept and observe them as fluctuations of energy without letting them pull you outward by fixating on other people, projecting into the future, or feeling sorry for yourself. If needed, use the Best Version of You (from Chapter Four) to make more conscious, non-reactive choices, while remaining self-aware.

- If your sense of otherness is too strong and you are pulled outward with intense negative emotions like anger, self-pity, or the desire to shut down, remember that you have the power to redirect your awareness back to your center at any time. Question the motivations behind your reactions: *"What am I so attached to?"* and *"What am I so afraid of?"* Listen to your inner voice, no matter how faint. Once you uncover the energy of your impulses, negative emotions will fade away.

- Make the effort to stay centered and detached, as an objective observer, to *steer clear of the roles you tend to assume without thinking* (the fixer, caretaker, pleaser, responsible, scapegoat, etc.). Stick to the Best Version of You to make choices while keeping an eye on your sense of otherness attempting to regain the control of your perception by setting you off-center with fear, anger, guilt, discomfort, a sense of gloom, or the need to justify yourself in any way.

- Watch your feelings and interactions closely to avoid getting hooked by the ego-octopus (from Chapter Seven). Be willing to "ride the wave of discomfort," as you stretch beyond your comfort zone by making new choices to break free from old roles, attitudes, and ideas. Although resistance is inevitable, it may not be immediately obvious, so remain alert to catch any negative thoughts, feelings, or events after you take steps toward greater self-expression and freedom.

• Try to watch your life-movie without being defensive or reactive. Every experience is an opportunity to get to know yourself better. *Accept life as it is, but be curious about what it is showing you about yourself.* Since it is a subconscious projection of familiar, outdated patterns and dynamics, you will not break free until you recognize how your interactions mirror a familiar yet distorted self-perception.

• Reflect on the energy behind your emotions and impulses, particularly any wounded needs driving them. Ask yourself, *"Is this my need to be right, heard, appreciated, useful, responsible, liked, or perfect?" "Is this my need to control, please, fight, judge, compete, hide, or seek validation?"* Observe yourself with compassion. Being aware of hidden motivations allows you to respond to your movie in a conscious manner instead of the usual fear-based or victim-blame interpretation of life centered on others and an egoic sense of deficiency.

• Use your breathing to drop any fear or pressure, as well as any attachment, to be able to choose the path of least resistance, trusting that everything is and will be the way it is meant to be. See yourself as a vehicle, not as a doer, and invest only the necessary energy to interact, find a solution, or tend to any issue without getting involved in anything other than the task at hand. Participate with full presence and focus, observing but also dismissing any negative charge from past, unresolved emotions that your sense of otherness brings forth if you are not anchored in yourself.

- Remind yourself that *everything in your life-movie is always about you* because there is no separation between you and your life—it is your perception and experience. Remain aware of *where and how you are directing your attention and energy*, and continue your self-reflection on your own after you have dealt with the external situation. With practice, however, you will be able to do it all as it is happening.

- Ask yourself: *"Why is this in my movie?" "What is it pointing out in me?"* and *"Why is it in my movie right now?"* These are the fundamental questions in the process that should come to mind as you navigate your day-to-day life, particularly when negative emotions arise. The purpose is not to find logical explanations or psychoanalyze things; it is to take spiritual responsibility for your tendencies and patterns of perception reflected in your reality by *turning your awareness from otherness to self*.

- Then delve more deeply into it: *"Who and what does this remind me of?"* Go down memory lane, as far as you can, to childhood situations where you recognize the figures and dynamics your sense of otherness is reflecting in your life now. Can you see your relationship with or between your father, mother, and siblings? Can you recall similar feelings or roles in other interactions? For instance, "I used to feel like this when my father would say this or that, or treat me like I didn't matter." "It reminds me of my mother's attitude toward me in these scenarios or of my parents' interaction in such and such situation." "I felt this way when my father, brother, sister ... did this to me." And so on.

- Make an effort to *connect the dots between the feelings triggered by your current reality and specific events in your past*, when you experienced something similar. When you do this, you will be able to see unresolved emotions in your patterns of perception and behavior. Do not generalize ("My parents 'always' did this or that"); recall specific situations to make clear connections to the past to release the emotional energy that got stuck there.

- Remember, this is your wounded child archetype tainting your experience of the present, so focus on you, not on what others did or didn't do, which can be a distraction; keep your attention inward to recognize old, repetitive feelings, beliefs, and attitudes reflected in your current reality. You are looking at the past to become aware of what you still believe about yourself that is causing you pain *now*.

- Focus on your feeling to *find the subconscious messages or themes in your movie arousing painful* emotions. Your feelings are your compass, so acknowledge them and listen to your inner voice to uncover which negative beliefs about yourself they are pointing at through the external situation. Examples of false ideas include: "I am not good enough." "I don't matter." "I am insignificant." "I am alone." "I am too different." "Someone or something else is always more important than me." "I am only valuable when I take care of others." "I am small." "I cannot take care of myself." "I am invisible." "I don't matter." "I am wrong or doing something wrong." "I am flawed." "Others will not like me if I am not perfect." "I am a child." "I need to be controlled." "I am worthless and don't deserve to express myself, enjoy life, or be happy, successful, independent ..." You get the idea.

- Again, *recognize the repetitive nature of these themes by recalling similar situations* throughout your life, going as far as you can remember. Investigate these patterns from all possible angles, like a detective—those that are obvious as well as those that show up in subtler ways, as negative internal chatter or your attitudes in relation to others. Do the Radical Honesty Process (from Chapter Five) to dig deeper, and the exercise to Retrieve Your Little Orphans (from Chapter Six), as needed. The goal is to make connections between your sense of otherness (the internalized voices and dynamics of the past) and the situations and feelings in your current experience.

- Whether these messages are overt or hidden, if they are in your life-movie, they are about you—about your beliefs and past impressions. The ego-mind will analyze, judge, and blame others to feel in control, but it is not really about them or their movie; *these are your patterns of self-perception* reflecting where your emotional energy is stuck and keeps revolving.

- Trust your intuition to identify them, along with any familiar, power-based dynamics that produce painful emotions, either through your interactions or your internal, self-defeating chatter. Check where your attention is, to *see how you are letting your inner bully take most of the room in your life-movie.* The more you fixate on others, the more *otherness* you allow and have to deal with from a wounded sense of self. Avoid judging or getting defensive, to uncover what your movie is pointing at in yourself that is distorting your experience.

• Once you are clear about these messages and themes, remind yourself that no matter how intense or painful your emotions may be, *your suffering comes from false ideas about yourself.* Thinking that others are causing them is how your ego-mind deters you from taking responsibility for your own happiness. Question their reality by asking, "*Is the idea that I am ... unloved, not good enough, insignificant, unheard, alone, responsible, etc., absolutely true, or is it based on a wounded need for validation?*" More importantly, "*Do I have to let this idea taint my experience, take away my joy, or disconnect me from this moment?*" and "*Can I give myself permission to experience it differently?*" The answer should be obvious, so rather than continuing to identify with it, *choose to disbelieve this false idea!* When you examine and stop clinging to outdated, painful thoughts, the emotions they produce will vanish into thin air and you will feel much freer.

• Then investigate these three aspects: "*What do I need to let go of?*" "*What do I need to nurture?*" and "*What do I need to develop in myself?*" Find creative ways to express and release what you are uncovering: old expectations, attachments, self-images, illusions, judgments, beliefs, fears, and so on. Give yourself permission to cry, journal, draw, paint, go for a run, dance it out of your system, talk to someone about it or to yourself in front of a mirror, or meditate to dissolve it. (You can also use the self-inquiry process you will learn in Chapter Nine.)

• Do anything that helps you release what is in your mental field without suppressing or rationalizing it; doing so just keeps the same emotional energy brewing within, causing disruptions inside and out. You cannot let go of what you cannot see, but your patterns unravel gradually, as they repeat in your movie and you are able to recognize them more and more clearly. Be patient, compassionate, and persistent, giving yourself time and space to grieve these aspects showing you your own lack of love.

- Also, *find the internal triggers activating your negative patterns*, which is why they are showing in your life-movie *now*. It is often something you are doing to break free from what you no longer want. If it goes against old roles and tendencies, your sense of otherness will resist or try to punish you for it. Look at recent events and choices to understand why your resistance got triggered and is now getting in your way, either through others or with your own emotions. This can also be something you observe, hear, read, or dream that pulls you emotionally into the past and snowballs into disruptive situations.

- Finally, focus on nurturing and developing the qualities that would counter old roles by strengthening your sense of self and bringing you closer to the Best Version of You. What do you need to value or take care of in yourself? Where should you invest more energy to stop promoting imbalanced, painful situations? What have you neglected in yourself that needs more attention? *What do you need to detach from to be more flexible and emotionally independent?* Where do you need firmer boundaries to stop identifying with other people's judgments or behavior?

- You know the revolving quality of the mind will make your patterns repeat, so *think of different ways to respond to them in the future*. Be prepared by building empowering inner resources with clarity and self-awareness. Imagine how you would have liked to respond in the past so you can choose to do that when similar situations arise, instead of reacting on autopilot. What could you do to regain your center as soon as you recognize them? What would you say or do to disrupt toxic dynamics without investing much emotional energy? In a nutshell: *How can you dismiss or give less room to your sense of otherness in your life-movie?* You may not know when or how, but you know these patterns will cycle back around. It is essential to recognize them to stop feeding them your energy.

• Once you comprehend how external interactions reflect internal dynamics between your sense of self and your sense of otherness (the past), you may balance them out by choosing to *focus on what connects you to yourself in the present*—your creative endeavors, projects, and goals, as well as your spiritual practices, self-care, and self-exploration.

• Avoid overprocessing or dwelling on past events and negative emotions. If you find yourself doing that, ask again, *"Why is this in my movie, and why now?"* The purpose here is uncovering past, unresolved emotions and hidden beliefs, not maintaining the identification with them. Whether in your head or in your external reality, your sense of otherness is relentless at disturbing your peace by disconnecting you from yourself. The key to a good life is leaving the past behind by taking full spiritual responsibility for the present!

If you commit to this process, in time it becomes second nature, and all these steps happen at once, through an immediate recognition, as self-awareness and detachment also increase. All you need to do to be happy and free is drop your false ideas and concepts about yourself by investigating them as they are reflected in your reality. You have to see them clearly before you can dismiss them, but you will get better at putting the pieces together until all the steps become seamless. Yes, you may get confused, you may forget things, you may slide back, and you may feel overwhelmed or discouraged, because you are going against a sense of otherness that lives with you every day and is continually trying to deter you from turning inward.

It is important to give yourself permission to *be who you are and where you are*, rather than thinking you should be ahead of yourself, which is exactly how your sense of otherness disturbs your process of individuation by taking your power away! It is okay to go at your own pace and make so-called mistakes; they are just experiences through which you learn something about yourself. You are attempting to give much more room to your sense of self in your life-movie by stretching beyond old, familiar dynamics, while fully embracing life, rather than fighting or resisting anything. Be willing to drop your righteous, perfectionistic self-images; they perpetuate a constrictive inner bully frozen in time.

This is like clearing a path through a thick jungle of ignorance; it gets easier as you keep going and the path opens up. As you invest less and less emotional energy in the external appearance of *otherness*, you will tend to what comes your way with the sincere desire to know yourself. You will stop trying to fix or control things and people, and instead experience life as a journey of self-discovery. The key is to remember that this is *your* life-movie, nobody else's, and that it is all about *you*. In other words, it is Consciousness making you conscious of yourself until you realize that you are Consciousness.

Your life provides everything you need to recognize and explore the ego-mind that creates dramas and pain. If you are disciplined, the Swan Method will transform your experience of reality, allowing you to be at peace with yourself and the world. You don't need specific conditions or things to be happy. You don't have to acquire or prove anything. You don't need to convince anyone to see things your way or try to control their behavior to meet your wounded needs. Your movie will spontaneously shift and keep shifting as you continue your inward journey, redirecting your attention *from otherness to self*, to uncover the meaning of your life.

There is nothing to force or fix; everything is exactly the way it is meant to be for you to let go, nurture, and develop what you need to dissolve your mental entrapment. It does require effort and patience, but the more committed you are to your process, the more guidance you will receive. Use any and every experience to keep growing, without ever underestimating your inner bully. It will try to block your path whenever you attempt to stretch beyond the familiar. You are here to express in body and mind who you are: the eternal Self in human form. The ego-mind overpowers you when it becomes a victim of itself and you identify with it through the illusion of *otherness*. You must investigate it to liberate yourself.

Be grateful for all your experiences, both pleasant and painful; for your dreams and desires as well as your difficulties; for the people with whom you have crossed paths, both friends and foes, lovers and haters; and for all the opportunities to appreciate the impermanence of material existence through your suffering. All of it has led you to the desire to transcend your pain. First, by comprehending that it is all your own doing—in your mind by your mind—and then focusing on your *un-doing*, to step back and give way to the true director of this mysterious dream of matter and Spirit.

As you integrate the Swan Method, you start leaving the past behind by dissolving the ego-mind. Then, as the drive for truth and inner peace grows stronger, the external world will gradually lose its appeal, and you will experience a more neutral state of *being*. Your life will shift from the constant identification with sensory desires to a growing eagerness for introspection and solitude. By questioning one mental distortion after another, peeling away one layer of ignorance after another, you will uncover the gradations of your existence: from the outer to the inner world; from *otherness* to self; and from the ego-self to the eternal Self.

Up until this point, I have explored the different elements of ordinary consciousness to give you a broader perspective on the nature and purpose of your life. I have examined the paradoxical essence of Divine Consciousness and the various aspects of the psyche that produce your reality as a personal life-movie. I have also clarified how the ego-mind controls the movie to give you individualized experiences, bringing forth karmic dynamics in need of resolution through the revolving patterns of your sense of otherness. Finally, I have explained why taking spiritual responsibility is how you break free from the self-created suffering that keeps you spinning in the past and trapped in the delusion of duality.

The next chapter aims to help you move beyond all of these mental concepts and labels to transcend your individuality and unveil the totality of the Self you are. What I have discussed until now supports your process of individuation, which is an essential aspect for emotional and spiritual maturity. But the ultimate purpose of your human journey is to abide beyond the mind, in Pure Awareness, where there is no separation or *otherness*. As you question your perception, to be fully present in life, you also cultivate the habit of redirecting your attention inward on an ongoing basis, which purifies the mind and makes room for Divine Consciousness to dissolve your identifications.

Spiritual freedom demands the effort to let go of what you cling to, what you resist, and what you believe yourself to be, to realize the absolute truth that you are and have always been free. It results from recognizing that nothing is separate from you unless you allow the ideas of *me* and *mine* to alienate you and distort this truth; that the ego-mind does not exist except as a collection of memories and impressions that dissolve when you investigate them; and that only the eternal Self, where everything appears and disappears, is real, while everything else is just thoughts with which you trap yourself in suffering.

THE GOAL:
SPIRITUAL FREEDOM

CHAPTER NINE

Awakening to Your True Self

The mind of a perfect man is like a mirror. It grasps nothing; it expects nothing. It reflects but does not hold.
— *Lao Tzu*

According to Greek mythology, in retaliation for the murder of his son, every nine years king Minos of Crete would send seven Athenian boys and seven Athenian girls to be devoured by the Minotaur, a half-man, half-bull monster trapped in the treacherous Labyrinth. One year, prince Theseus volunteered to take the place of one of the boys, with the intention to kill the Minotaur and end this horrific practice.

On his arrival in Crete, he met princess Ariadne, who fell in love with him and gave him a sword and a clew of yarn to find his way out of the maze. After slaying the monster, Theseus followed the thread he had tied at the entrance and managed to escape with the young Athenians as well as Ariadne and her sister Phaedra, who later became his wife.

The ship Theseus used for this and other heroic endeavors was sent every year to the island of Delos, in honor of Apollo, and then kept in the harbor as a memorial. To preserve the ship, whenever a plank showed signs of decay, it was replaced with stronger timber. This raised the philosophical question as to whether the vessel that was being slowly renovated would still be considered the Ship of Theseus.

One could argue that replacing even one plank changed the ship, or that there was not one ship but as many as the number of boards being replaced, because each new plank altered its previous state. One could also reason that, even if a single original plank remained, then it would still be the same ship; that, regardless of how many planks were replaced, and whether these changes happened over time or all at once, the vessel would stand as the fundamental Ship of Theseus.

This paradox reflects the nature of your spiritual journey as well. Although it refers to a material object, the fact that you base your existence on something as temporary and changeable as your body and mind justifies the analogy. Furthermore, your self-discovery is an adventure from and to Divine Consciousness—paradoxical in itself—that demands a gradual transformation where each step in the process expands your perception. Every insight supersedes a previous level of understanding, offering new possibilities to engage with reality from a place of greater truth and authenticity.

Life is a dynamic force in constant fluctuation, and so is the mind-body complex you hold on to as a fixed identity. It wavers and changes, even if this may not be immediately apparent because, as with the famous vessel, what changes is of the same nature as what was there before, giving continuity to your self-perception. For instance, your cells are being replaced on an ongoing basis, at varying rates, so your body isn't exactly what it was a few weeks or months ago; these changes become more noticeable over time, as you get older. Your physical appearance, roles, goals, priorities, and all the aspects that give you the sense of being this particular "person" also undergo many modifications.

Like the Ship of Theseus, which represents memories of great achievements, your ego-mind is shaped with thoughts and impressions from past experiences. These are not who you are; they are who you *think* you are. That is, ideas you identify with on account of past events, memories, and desires, which also change. You believed to be a child and a teenager while growing up, and later you began to perceive yourself as an adult. Now you continue to age, knowing that your body is bound to die at some point. How could any of these temporary stages—the child, the teenager, the adult, the old person—be the real you?

And yet, your essential *being* prevails, untouched, beyond all your fluctuations and transformations, because you are the Pure Awareness that makes them real; nothing exists without your cognizance of it. You are constantly reacting to the world, on account of your past, but the world is a reflection of Consciousness in your mind that is perceived by the very Consciousness you are. The Self is projected as ego, and the ego creates the world. This is like a shadow play in which the Self is the light where everything happens and the ego-mind is what blocks the light to produce the shadow figures to which you get attached and with which you identify. These shadows disappear when you shed light onto them. The Self is beyond both light and darkness, but I use this analogy to point out the contrast between the Pure Awareness you are and the ignorance of the truth that you believe yourself to be.

All your troubles result from your desire for gratification and validation through your relationships, social success, money, and so on; they all arise or exist in the ego-mind, and only in the ego-mind. Until you relinquish this false I-sense, it will continue distorting your essential nature, dictating how you react to people and things. Its inherent self-centeredness produces the idea that life should revolve around your needs and desires, which creates conflicts and suffering. By pushing negative impressions and tendencies of perception, it prevents you from being fully present, anchored in its flow. You diminish this egoism with humility and devotion to something bigger than you or by investigating the ego to remove the ignorance it perpetuates.

The original purpose of the mind is to experience and then break free from its own creation—the world—which is an illusion. When it realizes the illusion, it develops dispassion toward its creation, thus eliminating the illusion and the suffering the illusion produces. Imagine yourself walking at night and suddenly seeing a shadow that looks like a snake. In that moment, you experience great fear and start thinking about what you can do to avoid being attacked; you may even feel paralyzed, believing that you are going to die. But if you look closely and realize that it is not a snake but a rope, then all your negative, painful thoughts instantly disappear. All you need to clear your mind is seeing the rope for what it really is.

Self-awareness, devotion, and dispassion (or non-attachment) purify the mind. Once it is cleared of false ideas, it becomes a vehicle of Divine Consciousness and no longer needs anything. Devotion removes the division produced by the ego; it is your internal, intimate connection to the Self or God—not somebody else's idea of God according to a religion, dogma, or scripture. Devotion is love for God, and God is your true Self. In this sense, all spiritual paths are essentially the same, because love and service for God is love and service for the Self. Also, love for the Self in you is love for the Self in all; it dissolves the distinction between "me" and "another" with which the ego hijacks the truth. The paths of devotion (*bhakti yoga*), selfless service (*karma yoga*), discipline (*raja yoga*), and Self-knowledge (*jnana yoga*) lead to the realization that everything appears, changes, and disappears in the Pure Awareness you are.

If you comprehend that your divine essence is steady peace and happiness, then there is nothing to seek outside of you. Your task consists in removing what obscures this truth, like clearing the clutter in a room to create more space. The space is there and has been there all along; it is the excessive number of objects that keep it hidden. Similarly, the ego-mind is the relentless flow of thoughts and desires cluttering your true nature. Since the ego is mobile and shape-shifting, removing the ignorance that hinders Self-realization takes earnest persistence.

Spiritual ignorance is either forgetfulness of the Self or the obstruction to the knowledge of the Self. In an advanced spiritual seeker, the imprints of discriminative wisdom previously achieved awaken spontaneously or by simply hearing the truth from a master. All ignorance is removed at once or within a short period. For most people, however, this is a long process, like climbing the Love-Consciousness Pyramid to purify the mind of attachment, egoism, and doubt. It requires hearing and reflecting on the truth repeatedly, while keeping the mind inwardly directed.

Hearing the truth opens you to question the illusions and false ideas of the ego-mind. Reflecting on the truth brings insight and discrimination. And withdrawing the mind gradually reveals the absolute reality of the Self. Without discipline and introspection, any insight may stagnate as intellectual knowledge without being actualized at the experiential level. If the truth stays in the mental realms, the ego can use it for its self-importance, by making people feel superior, or to manipulate others to gain validation or gratification. While hiding in plain sight, the ego continues to control the perception and behavior, thus defeating the real purpose of knowing the truth.

Although not really separate, there appear to be two parallel realities within manifest Consciousness. One is the Supreme Self dreaming a dream yet unperturbed by it, and the other the limited perception of the ego as the temporary *experiencer* of life blocking the awareness of its real nature. You are dreaming a dream within a dream as your life-movie, imagining things and people to be different and separate from you. In reality, objects appear and disappear without your control, fashioned by the elements and *gunas* that keep the dream in motion. But just like water is water, even if it takes the shape of different containers, and light is light regardless of the many colors and figures it brings out, your essence is absolute and remains untouched, beyond its myriad appearances and modifications.

The ego seeks pleasure through sensory perception, and the ephemeral quality of physical experience produces pain. In time, pain brings the recognition of your limitations, giving way to humility, and devotion, as you take responsibility for your perception and behavior. Complete surrender comes from understanding that what causes you suffering is the self-centered idea of being separate—of being a "person" judging and comparing to other "persons"—and that this idea constricts you to a false identity based on mere mental concepts.

When you are deeply asleep, you are at peace and need nothing. You are happy because you are not conscious of your existence, but as soon as you wake up, your I-sense becomes active, producing a constant flow of thoughts and cravings. You cannot experience the peace and joy found in dreamless sleep or in deep meditation without rejecting this false identity. Its desires and thoughts perpetuate your dissatisfaction and suffering. However, just like individual consciousness fades away when you are asleep, the ego-mind recedes when you redirect it inward.

The ultimate goal of your human adventure is purifying the mind until your true Self perceives itself apart from the ego. This is a gradual process that starts with indifference for the truth as a result of ignorance and egoism. Then it fluctuates, going from indifference to confusion, and from confusion to intellectual understanding. In due course, your understanding and reflection of the truth manifest as experience. Finally, when your experience of the truth becomes steady, it leads to Self-realization, once the illusion of individuality disappears. Real freedom is freedom from your identifications, since your attachments and fears keep you trapped in a limited experience of life, under the control of the ego-mind that isolates you from the totality you are.

Every experience offers you these possibilities: you can accept or enjoy it in the present; you can resist it, which causes you pain; and you can get attached to it, which produces expectations and desires that eventually result in pain as well. Your best choice is to openly embrace every moment, whether it is pleasant or painful, engaging with it as a *witness* by refusing the sense of ownership the ego fabricates. Clearly, this requires self-discipline to dis-identify from it at every opportunity to gain inner peace.

You hold on to the illusions of the external world in the hopes of liberating yourself from the suffering they create, like a dog chasing its tail, because you have mistaken joy for sensory pleasure, love for attachment or lust, and wisdom for intellectual understanding. But the main goal of a spiritual seeker is to quiet the mind—to transition from the verbal to the non-verbal. From sound to silence. From the usual mental-emotional fluctuations to the stillness of Pure Awareness. In this sense, true spiritual growth can be gauged by the degree of inner silence, rather than by the accumulation of concepts. That is, how long you are able to concentrate on a single thought, free from other, uninvited thoughts. The tendency of the ego-mind is the opposite. You start reclaiming your essential freedom when you let go of the familiar roller coaster of thoughts, desires, and experiences with which you identify, based on the belief that you are nothing without them.

You become conscious of the world reflected on your mind, but you need silence to become aware that you are aware—or rather, that you are Awareness. Being fully present in the moment is a portal into your eternal, infinite nature beyond space or time. When the mind is away from its usual preoccupations, the flow of light and love underlying everything is revealed in you as silence, as inner peace. Awareness is silent, underlying all intellectual cognizance. Silence is the backdrop of existence and the stillness that dissolves ego. It is not the avoidance or absence of external sound but the suspension of thought waves, which is the real meaning of *yoga*: the union with the Divine.

The ancient sages of India perceived sound as the movement of energy and the cause of Creation. If there is any change in nature, it produces a sound; it can be as loud as thunder, as quiet as the buzzing of a bee, and as subtle as your breathing. Silence exists beyond time, space, and causation, while sound disturbs the absolute, eternal reality of the Self with the thoughts, words, and concepts we use to communicate and interact with those we perceive as separate from ourselves.

Sound originates from silence, then it creates thoughts and speech; in turn, speech connects us to the world with ideas, feelings, and desires leading to actions. It maintains the illusion of duality through the perception of the ego-mind as subject and object—the sense of self and the sense of otherness reflected on the outside. The mind is always talking, except in deep sleep and meditation, where this illusion of individuality and separation fades away. When speech ceases internally, the *otherness* dissolves and silence gives rise to Oneness. In this sense, silence is the language of the Self or God.

You are wrapped in silence during deep sleep, but as soon as you wake up, you start thinking; then the flow of thoughts continues throughout the day. If you pay close attention, however, you can appreciate that *Awareness always precedes thought*; it abides beyond the ordinary consciousness constrained by judgments and labels. In the same way that you can use a flashlight in a dark room to discern what is in the room, Pure Awareness gives reality to the objects you perceive when it is reflected on your mind as your consciousness. Nothing exists without it. It is from the center of your being that the world comes to be. Although the ego-mind hijacks your light with names and categories as it fixates on external objects, it is from the center of your being that the world comes to be.

The mind keeps the dream of the world alive, and the world keeps the mind active. By turning it inward, you access the stillness that dissolves the fluctuations that cause confusion and suffering through the illusion of separation. Spiritual awakening is the realization that what appeared to be an object is in fact the subject—the Inner Self orchestrating your personal movie within a collective dream of appearances. If you stop focusing on your *otherness* and direct your attention to examine the ego-mind, you gain access to the real subject and director of your life.

The Self cannot be defined. The certainty of *being* transcends all identities that waver and change. The Self is the One hearing through your ears, seeing through your eyes, experiencing and feeling its existence through you. It is not separate from anything, yet it is not affected by anything. The ego-mind, on the other hand, needs to give things a form, a name, a label, or an image to differentiate them from each other. It is helpless if you relinquish those ideas to live in a fluid state of *presence*, here and now, watching people and objects come and go without resisting or clinging to any of them.

When you anchor in the eternity of the present, you comprehend that you are neither the subject nor the object, although both exist in you. You are the space where everything unfolds. You are not in the world, the world is in you—or rather, *the world is you*. Because you are, everything is. The consciousness "I am" is the center from which everything emerges: life as you see it as well as the ideas that life continues when you don't see it. Your physical body may be in the material world and of the material world, but you are not. It can be asleep or in a coma without your perception of the world, because the whole universe arises with your consciousness.

The paradox of manifest Consciousness is that it is both real and illusory, eternal and temporary, still and ever-changing, made of Spirit and matter, of Self and ego. The externalized mind is your field of experience. It can be restricted by introversion or inwardness and get absorbed back into your spiritual heart, which is the true source of all experience. This is where the Self abides and whence the *I-am-ness* and the ego originate, as well as the elements and qualities of nature, and all forms and mental-emotional fluctuations. As you tend to your karma through the demands of your life-movie, you must keep the mind inwardly directed by anchoring your attention in your heart, in the consciousness "I am."

You are fully present and aware when you are centered and detached, and as you develop dispassion for the world, you recognize it as a dream. However, being still long enough to perceive life as a dream triggers massive resistance. The idea of not having control or free will means losing your identity as the *doer*, so the ego-mind will keep spinning in the intellectual knowledge of the truth while blocking its realization for as long as possible. You may even think that being still or mentally quiet means being inert, because you are so identified with the fluctuations of your mind that it is hard to imagine life without them. And yet, peace and clarity emerge only when the mind is quiet. You will still achieve what you are meant to, as per your destiny, but with a quiet mind you will go about it like an actor playing various roles without ever losing sight that it is a play.

Inner silence is at the core of every spiritual path aiming for liberation. The path of devotion quiets the mind through worship and rituals, trusting and surrendering the egoic will to Divine Will. The path of selfless action subdues the mind by removing any self-interest to serve God by serving others. The path of discipline cultivates stillness with a variety of methods, including breath control, sense withdrawal, concentration, and meditation to achieve superconscious states. And the path of Self-knowledge dissolves the mind by either examining it to diminish its activity or seeking its source to remove the delusion of separation from the Self.

Since they share the same goal, these paths tend to overlap. Of course, your ego-mind will believe *yours* is better than other ones, but they all emerge from and lead back to Consciousness, for everything is Consciousness. Rather than wasting your energy judging or comparing, which keeps you fixated on the *otherness* that alienates you, accept where you are and what rings true to you, trying to break free from all divisions as you get to know yourself by observing and inquiring into your life-movie.

If you cultivate self-awareness to drop your attachments, aversions, and fears, you start seeing things and people for what they are and embracing life as it is. An internal openness happens, making more room for Pure Awareness to erase your ignorance and limited, dream-like existence. In the initial stages, you may search for the cause of your distress with some type of counseling, reading books, or joining groups in search of tools and support. But if you don't delve deeply within on an ongoing basis, you run the risk of establishing familiar, outdated dynamics of *otherness* with the groups or people with whom you interact.

The key is to remember that this is your movie! No matter how spiritually oriented the people in your life may be, they will mirror your patterns of perception, both positive and negative. You cannot escape this. Until the mind becomes clear and undisturbed, what appears on the outside is your ego. You see others as separate persons because you consider yourself a person, or a mind-body, rather than an expression of Consciousness. When you reject this and other ideas upholding the perception of the world as separate from you, your experience of life transforms into love.

If instead of getting involved in the typical power dynamics and drama of the ego, you recognize your life-movie as your projection, and the world as a bigger reflection of it, you can examine what keeps you (and the world) out of balance and in discontent. Dispassion and self-awareness turn your experience into a meditative space of Pure Awareness. Meditation must become a way of *being*, not just a daily practice to diminish the flow of thoughts or reach superconscious states. Although a daily discipline is vital to master the ego-mind, it should continue during all your worldly activities through inwardness, mindfulness, and non-attachment.

The mind is a collection of thoughts, memories, and desires that will not persist if you see them for what they are: mere ideas and emotional fluctuations disconnecting you from the present, which is where you regain access to your true Self. When you are busy running after your desires, you seek pleasure to avoid the distress inherent in the egoism and ignorance of your ego-mind, but you fail to recognize that your own desires and attachments arouse the negative emotions that prompt you to chase desires. It's a vicious loop of ego entrapment.

When you choose to be indifferent to both pleasure and pain, neither expecting nor refusing anything, while keeping your attention at the center of your being, you experience happiness as your nature and realize that you have been disturbing it by looking for some particular experience of it. To shift such ingrained perception, you must consciously refuse all sense of egoic doership and ownership—that is, the identification with your body and mind that creates the idea of *me* and *mine*, and therefore the division between you and *others*.

You will feel uncertain and vulnerable for a while, as you open up to life as it happens without expecting it to bring you some kind of material or spiritual benefit. It is the self-centered, greedy nature of your ego that fixates on appearances to create the illusion of security. You heal this persistent sense of deficiency by removing all fears and expectations until you realize that you are One with All. If you are everything you perceive, then what is there to desire or to be afraid of? But if you continue to cling to your desires and the external power dynamics of *otherness*, the outward pull will be too strong to simply *be* the Pure Awareness you are. When you surrender to life as a play of Consciousness, with total faith in the Divine, your needs will be taken care of.

Self-realization is continuous, uninterrupted Self-awareness. Awareness is not an experience; it is the backdrop that makes any experience possible—the timeless essence of every experience. Just like your eyes cannot see themselves without a reflective surface, Pure Awareness is not aware of itself until it is reflected as individual consciousness, granting you the cognitive ability to perceive, act, react, and direct your attention. When the egoic sense of experience is gone, as in deep sleep or superconscious states, your true Self prevails. Even if it happens by Grace, your effort is never in vain. Once you become a *witness* to life by removing the idea of being the doer, you will attain your divine destiny regardless of the path you have chosen.

In truth, you are the path, the traveler, and the destination—the eternal Self beyond creation, time, space, or suffering. Don't waste your time expecting some epiphany or comparing yourself to other people; these are distractions of your ego. Your biggest mistake has been believing that what is in you is outside of you, through your projection of *otherness*, and that what appears outside of you is in you, through your identification with sensory perception. Mental fluctuations are external and impermanent, yet you have taken them to be the real you. That is, you have objectified your existence, thinking the world is a tangible, separate reality, when it is just a projection and reflection of your psyche. This is your most fundamental confusion, and it has brought you immense sorrow.

Your mind and body are subject to karmic events through the elements and qualities of nature, but you have the choice to either identify with sensory perception or to be a witness to it. You know you are you. You never doubt this, not even if your relationships or roles end, or if your attachments and self-images change. This *I-am-ness* is undeniable, since you can only be absolutely certain that *you are*. All other ideas about yourself and other people change or rely on something external that changes as well. They are temporary thoughts.

If you stop identifying with such thoughts as, "I am this or that," or conditions like, "I am valuable only when others see me as valuable," what remains is who you really are and have always been, beyond any concepts. Everything arises from and brings you back to this essential *I-am-ness* as the source of your experience. It persists through the fluctuating states you undergo each day, through the various stages of your life, and throughout the cycles of your soul journey. It is from here that your existence takes shape as your ego consciousness.

When you fall asleep, the outer world fades away, but the *I-am-ness* is present in your dreams and in the dreamless state. Dreams are a mix of memories, desires, fears, and imaginations symbolized by different characters and situations. They are all about you; you are the main character, even without any external input. When you wake up, the dream vanishes and ordinary consciousness returns. You are aware of your body and physical senses again, as well as the shift between the dream and wakeful states, because your *I-am-ness* is as present in the dream as when you are awake. It is the only constant, the thread that gives continuity to your individual existence.

While you are dreaming, your subconscious content comes to the surface without the filtering of the ego-mind; this makes your dreams seem disconnected and absurd until you explore their symbolic meaning. In truth, the dream state is not different from the waking state, except that it is shorter and usually disrupted; but both are made of the same material in your causal body. You become more of a yogi in deep, dreamless sleep, when there is no mental activity or consciousness of the other states, so any sense of individual experience is absent. Although brief, it is a meditative state in Pure Awareness.

This pause in consciousness makes you feel that each day is new. It is a restful, pleasant break from the ego-mind during which you relax into simply *being* while your physical body recharges. Although you are not conscious, you are the happiest in this state, devoid of thoughts. Each moment offers you the opportunity to abide beyond the mind, but in the wakeful state it requires discipline because you are bombarded with thoughts that you follow blindly, fixating on the outer world to satisfy the needs of your ego.

As a spiritual seeker, however, your aim is to attain the same peaceful state of deep sleep while being awake, which you achieve by dismissing your false I-sense to allow your true nature to take over. When your eternal Self arises as ego, it gets camouflaged, so you perceive yourself as separate from your own totality. But everything happens in the field of Consciousness, for and by Consciousness, although none of its manifestations are conscious in themselves; they merely reflect the light of Consciousness, like the moon reflects the light of the sun.

The sun isn't affected by its reflection on the moon, and the Self isn't affected by its modifications on your mind. The light of the moon allows you to see things at night, but you don't need it when the sun is visible. Similarly, the ego-mind is useful in the world while you undergo and explore your human existence; it loses its purpose when you remove the ignorance blocking your inner light. You wouldn't take the reflection of the sun on the moon for the sun, and yet you take external, sensory appearances for your true nature.

God and the Self are one, so wherever you are, God is; and wherever God is, you are as well. There is no separation, although your perception gets tainted by the delusion of duality. Because the ego-mind traps you in this imaginary division, spiritual freedom requires a reverse process, or involution, from the multiplicity of forms and the ideas of *me* and *mine* back to the Oneness of Divine Consciousness. That is, again, from *otherness* to self, and from the ego-self to the eternal Self.

Taoism expresses this in simple terms: the ultimate Reality fades when openness turns into spirit, spirit turns into energy, and energy turns into form, which leads to greed and destruction. Returning to the eternal, unifying Reality entails forgetting form to cultivate energy, forgetting energy to cultivate spirit, and forgetting spirit to cultivate openness, where everything flows freely. Duality disappears in spontaneous, effortless action—or *non-action*—when there is no attachment or resistance to any aspect of life, either material or subtle. Holding on to anything constricts your essence, and this is what causes you suffering.

You view your identity as your mind-body, but both body and mind are transitory tools with which you can experience the world of appearances and then also transcend the world. Your body is a creation of the ego that dies once it reaches its karmic timeline. Your mind or subtle body is bound to die when you develop the discriminative wisdom leading to your Liberation, after innumerable experiences and births. Eventually, your causal body will also merge back with the Cosmic Mind after your last incarnation. If you pierce through the layers of the soul by clearing the greedy, self-centered qualities of the ego, your sense of self transforms into a *sattvic* self, or *no-self*.

In Zen, this process has been described as mastering a bull, since the ego is just as strong, stubborn, and defensive but can also be subdued with discipline and patience. When you first start searching for the bull, you discover its footprints. By following them, you find the bull, which you must catch with a rope so it will not wander away looking for grass. Once you have caught it, it needs to be tamed, using the rope and a whip to ride it home. At home, both of you can rest; you don't need the whip or the rope anymore, because the bull cannot go outside. Then, in silent contemplation, you go beyond the illusion of the bull being an external object and of yourself being the subject mastering it.

In yoga, the awakening of wisdom takes place in states of *samadhi*, or superconsciousness, when the concentration on one thought dissolves all other thoughts along with the original thought. This leads to the perception of the nature of reality. If these states are sustained, the ego then becomes the focus of concentration. As a result, a blissful phase emerges to further clear the mind, revealing the ego as the original cause of the modifications of Consciousness through the elements and qualities of nature.

If such transcendental states continue, discrimination and wisdom increase, bringing about the awareness of the Self as the source of the ego while dissolving it in the process. Finally, if higher levels of *samadhi* become steady, full knowledge is achieved in non-duality, as the causal seeds of perception carrying false concepts burn in the fire of Pure Awareness. The ego disappears when the Self sees the mind as separate from itself, thus removing the false identification and realizing itself as the totality of existence.

This is the ultimate goal of all human life. It is what my analogy of reaching the top of the Love Consciousness Pyramid referred to, which is not really going anywhere or climbing anything; it is simply refusing to identify with the ego-mind that creates all sorts of illusions to block the truth of who you are. Only at this level of complete purity, when all ignorance and egoism are cleared, can an enlightened soul participate in the world without falling into delusion or temptation again.

It demands dispassion, which develops by restraining the ego-mind from its usual desires for sense objects, as a result of recognizing the pain those desires invariably lead to. You don't have to live in a cave or a monastery to cultivate this desirelessness, although periods of solitude and contemplation can certainly speed up the process. You may tend to your daily responsibilities while being increasingly self-aware, examining the ego-mind at every opportunity to know yourself. You may concentrate on one thought to exclude all other thoughts, which can also be the thought of God as the essence of devotion. And you may also seek the source of all your mental activity, which takes you directly to the Self from which everything arises.

Life is a play of Divine Consciousness, a multilayered game of self-awareness. To see it for what it is, you need to be fully present, anchored in your heart. Ordinary reality is impermanent and changeable, while the Self is the only absolute and timeless Reality, shining by its own light. Pure Awareness emerges when you stop blocking it with false ideas of who you think you are or should be, and who you think others should be as well. Your effort consists in removing the distorted perception that hides the truth.

When you surrender to life, you experience peace. Think of a tree. Animals and insects find shelter in it or eat the leaves and fruits it produces. People may lean against it, cool off under its shade, climb it to see something at a distance, or tie a swing on a branch for the enjoyment of children. They can also use it to hang another human being. Regardless, the tree leads a quiet life, serving innumerable beings yet totally unconcerned with its usefulness. Try to be like a tree, generous with your presence and what you have to offer but free from any attachment, self-interest, or self-images. Be a witness to life as it happens, mindfully participating instead of just reacting to it. Remain aware of yourself at all times; being aware is being awake.

You suffer because of your self-centeredness and egoism. You feel anger, self-pity, frustration, loneliness, and the whole collection of negative emotions because you expect the world to make you happy by satisfying the constant flow of desires produced by your ego-mind. In addition, you see others as separate from you, which creates judgments, comparisons, and fears. It is not the world that causes your negative emotions; it is your tainted perception and your resistance to accepting life as it is, without clinging to its pleasurable aspects while rejecting the unpleasant ones.

You don't need external validation to find fulfillment. You don't have to be important to be happy. You don't need special powers to be spiritual. These are illusions that only serve the needs of the ego and disconnect you from your true Self. The steady peace and love you yearn for are already within you as the real you; to reclaim them, you have to restrain the outward pull of the mind. You are a point of light, an eternal spark or expression of Pure Awareness, as well as its witness. The Self becomes aware of itself through its reflection as your human consciousness, but there is no real separation between you, others, the world, or the Divine.

Removing this false division demands dropping all your false ideas to realize that we all are but appearances of Consciousness reflecting one another in the field of Consciousness. If you remain detached, anchored in your heart, you become one with the flow of life in the eternity of the present moment. The key is refusing to follow the constant activity of the ego-mind that clutters your perception, which takes discipline and humility. The ego is mobile and shape-shifting, while the Self is still. And yet, as long as you identify with your sensory perception and the illusion of *otherness*, the Self proves even more elusive.

When you feel attraction, aversion, or fear toward other people or objects, your essential *I-am-ness* gets tainted. There is no way to simply *be* if you are constantly reacting to your life-movie as a result of past, unresolved emotions. However, if you recognize that all your painful emotions are mere reflections of distorted *ideas* about yourself, you stop giving them your power and they vanish into thin air. But you have to see the core ideas behind your negative emotions to remove what fuels them, rather than believing something external is causing them. Your identifications make them seem real and solid, but they dissolve as soon as you see them for what they are.

If you implement the Swan Method on an ongoing basis, questioning your life-movie to uncover the patterns of perception that keep you in the past, you will dismiss outdated beliefs hindering your experience of reality while training your mind to turn inward. Once this inward direction becomes natural, your introspection will spontaneously take you more deeply within, to the source of all your mental-emotional fluctuations. The process is similar to feeling constricted inside a box and trying to push the walls to make more room for yourself. You keep stretching the box as your perception expands. The box gets bigger and bigger until it eventually disappears and you realize there was never a box; you were trapped in your false ideas, struggling with a painful reality you created with your thoughts.

The self-inquiry process below will help you dissolve this mental entrapment. Do it as a daily meditation and during your ordinary activities. It expands the Anchoring in the Consciousness "I Am" meditation from Chapter Seven, so it starts with it before delving more deeply within. This is an advanced approach that may seem difficult at first, but it is the most direct path to remove the ego and achieve true freedom.

* * *

Living in Pure Awareness

For your daily practice, choose a spot where you won't be interrupted, and sit in a relaxed, steady position with your eyes closed. Briefly acknowledge anything that draws your attention by labeling it but without dwelling on it: "Tension ... restlessness ... noise ... memories ... pressure ... heat ..." or any other thoughts and sensations that may surface. Then take a deep breath to drop them all, consciously choosing to leave anything external out.

Now bring your attention to your breathing, focusing on the air going in and out with the mantra *Soham* (or *Hamsa*) for a few minutes. Inhale *So*, and exhale *Ham*, following the natural, rhythmic sound of your breathing: *So ... Ham ... So ... Ham ... So ... Ham ...* Once the mind slows down, direct your awareness and your breathing to your heart, turning *Soham* into "I am." Do not follow the breath going in and out anymore; instead, imagine it going in and in, into your center, settling in the thought, "I am." Breathe in "I" and breathe in "am." *I ... Am ... I ... Am ... I ... Am ...* The breath will become subtler as your concentration increases and your mind quiets down.

Anchor your attention in your heart, relaxing into "I am" without following any other thoughts. While staying centered, mentally step back for a moment, bringing your awareness a few inches behind and above your body to observe yourself. Watch yourself breathing, sitting, meditating. There is no cognitive thought here, just an awareness, a *feeling*. You may be using your imagination for this now, but if you continue with this practice, the Inner Witness or Seer will be increasingly apparent, and you will engage with the world from this neutral place as well, observing the play of Consciousness unfold on its own.

Stay in Pure Awareness, attentive to the One who is beyond body, mind, and ordinary consciousness, completely present and still, while you concentrate on "I am" to exclude everything else. If any other, uninvited thoughts arise, inquire:

"Who is having these thoughts?"
and
"Who is aware of these thoughts?"

Focus on the source of awareness rather than the thoughts. Whether images, emotions, sensations, or ideas come up, they don't matter right now. Redirect your energy and attention to your heart, away from any mental, external activity, by letting the most natural answer draw you back in:

"I am."

Stay with the "I am" at the center of your being, letting all other thoughts fade away. Relax into it, using your breathing, while also aware of the Seer or Inner Witness. "I am" is not an experience; it is a *feeling*, a certainty that is internal and ever present. Anchor in your heart with this certainty of simply *being* here and now, by refusing to follow any mental activity; thoughts will fade away if you don't cling on to them. Once immersed in the feeling "I am," inquire:

"Who am I?"

Then let the question take you even more deeply within by following the thought, "I-I" inward. "I-I" is where the ego "I" and the eternal "I" meet. Stay in the neutral flow of "I-I" without resisting or inviting any other thoughts to question or analyze it. Trust and surrender completely, letting it take you beyond the mind. "I-I" will gradually fade, and the mind and your I-sense will dissolve in Pure Silence. Remain in Silence, in Stillness. Become the Silence. Become the Stillness. Become the infinite Space where they merge.

If thoughts or sensations distract you, take a deep breath and inquire again, as many times as needed, "Who is aware of these thoughts?" to regain your center, bringing your attention back to the "I am." Then continue inquiring, "Who am I?" and follow the "I-I" inward. This must be the single-pointed thought that removes all other thoughts to lead you to the source from which your whole world emerges. Go back to it over and over until the ego-mind surrenders. In summary, the direction of your awareness should be from *So Ham* to "I am," and further inward from "Who am I?" to "I-I" to let Consciousness (Silence) take over, even if momentarily, until it becomes steady.

You can find a guided version of this self-inquiry meditation at: YouAreYourHealer.com/self-inquiry-meditation.

Once you start coming back into the world, gently open your eyes while staying in this neutral state, in this divine Space, before going back to your usual activities. Try to maintain it as you go on with your day, remaining mindful and centered, and continue with the self-inquiry with your eyes open.

Inquiring, "Who am I?" is not an intellectual exercise to satisfy the mind with concepts and labels, but the sincere investigation into the very source of your mental identifications. In this sense, it is closer to pondering, "What is this false 'I' that I believe myself to be?" Similarly, the intention behind the question,

"Who is having (or thinking) these thoughts?" is more like, "Whence do these thoughts arise?" to seek their source.[1] Don't expect to find answers from another little "self" hidden somewhere to keep your false, egoic identity active. "Who am I?" is the most important question of your human journey; it eliminates all other questions and then disappears as well, like individual waves disappear by merging with the ocean.

Staying in the consciousness "I am" draws you inward, and questioning this *I-am-ness* dissolves your false ego-sense in its source. It takes a long time, so be consistent, patient, and earnest, using the Swan Method to clear your path for self-inquiry. This is not just another meditation practice; it gives you the most direct access to your Inner Self. Continue the process throughout the day, with your eyes open, redirecting the mind inward as you tend to your life-movie.

Check in with yourself: *"Where is my attention?"* at all times; turn your awareness from *otherness* to self, and continue further in that inward direction, remaining detached but intensely self-aware, as you ponder:

"Who is walking ... smiling ... speaking ... cooking ... eating ... writing ... listening ... sitting ... working ... reacting ... (etc.)?"

Use this technique as well whenever you experience painful emotions or thoughts:

---

[1] The Indian sage Ramana Maharshi introduced self-inquiry as *Nan Yar*, which can be translated as "I" (*nan*) "who?" (*yar*) or "Who am I?" Investigating this fundamental question helps us dissolve the sense of individuality or separation that creates our suffering. The self-inquiry process shared here is based on Ramana's teachings.

"Who is feeling pain ... anger ... disappointment ... sadness ... shame ... loneliness ... jealousy ... fear ... (etc.)?"

and

"Who is aware of this?"

"I am."

Anchor yourself in the "I am" while keeping some of your awareness slightly above you and the situation you are in, to access the Seer that watches everything. This brings you to a neutral state of *witnessing*, or simply *being*. Relax here, with full presence, while tending to the task at hand. That is, acting without reacting, observing and accepting life as it is, without letting the ego-mind disconnect you from your true nature. With discipline and determination, your perception will transform, and you will increasingly abide in the Pure Awareness you are, until you realize that nothing is ever separate from you.

Cultivating inwardness through the Swan Method makes it easier to give continuity to this process and maintain a neutral state until it becomes stable. As self-inquiry turns steady, the mind gives up trying to hijack or cover up the Self. You will experience greater peace, viewing the world with curiosity and dispassion, and feeling spontaneously driven to act without seeking validation, gratification, or credit. Your clarity and insight will also increase as you master the ego-mind and allow love and light to guide you. You don't have to change or fix anything; just remain in this truth, connected to life in the fluidity of the present moment.

* * *

To wrap up this guide, I'd like to leave you with a few statements, which I may explore further in a future publication, as a reminder to go beyond the ordinary perception that drowns Pure Awareness with a flood of thoughts and desires. Reflect on them regularly, with the earnest desire to pierce through the delusion of being separate or deficient in any way, questioning the reality of your ego-mind to transcend the duality or *otherness* that causes you suffering.

1. Creation is a dream of the Self, a fluid play of Divine Consciousness continuously unfolding to experience itself as infinite qualities, forms, and attributes, including the cosmos, nature, the human mind, and all possible realms of existence, activity, and experience. These are all expressions of the One eternal Self you are.

2. Only Consciousness is real, for nothing else is permanent or conscious in itself. When the mind comes out of the Self, the world appears. As long as the world appears to be real, through the fluctuations of the mind, the Self remains hidden. When all mental activity stops, the Self emerges as your true, eternal essence.

3. Because the mind is made of thoughts, there is no world apart from thoughts. The thought "I am" is the source of all other thoughts, but "I am my body and mind" is the idea that causes all human misery. It arises from the ignorance and egoism of a false I-sense that isolates you from the totality of existence. Body and mind are vehicles or tools for the Self to experience its dreamworld and then awaken from it.

4. The I-thought or ego is the principle of individuality that creates a sense of separation between "self" and "other," thus

breeding greed, power struggles, and destruction. It holds an ingrained sense of deficiency because it obstructs Pure Awareness with the delusion of duality and the polarizing ideas that instigate conflict and pain.

5. The mind is a revolving collection of memories and impressions producing a constant flow of desires and thoughts, including the different beliefs about God, the soul, the world, time, space, life, and death. Tainted with the ignorance of the ego, it creates experiences and illusions based on the idea of being a unique person, separate and different from others.

6. As an impermanent concept, the mind is unreal, and anything perceived by it is also impermanent or unreal, just like the characters and situations in your dreams. The persistent investigation of the mind leads to the realization that all events are experiences of the Self, witnessed by the Self, yet never affecting or disturbing the Self in any way.

7. Only a state of neutrality or inner peace allows you to recognize that suffering is of the ego-mind alone. It is caused by negative tendencies of perception built with erroneous ideas you believe and reinforce about yourself that revolve in the reality that reflects them. That is, the world appears as you think yourself to be.

8. When the mind is disturbed, all you can see is your ego and its mental-emotional fluctuations. If you identify with it, you become the *doer*, the *experiencer*, and the *sufferer* trapped in a painful life-movie made of false, unconscious beliefs. You release your attachment to them through self-knowledge or intense devotion.

9. The ego is not conscious and cannot know or heal itself. Its very nature is to attend to external objects—through the sense of duality or *otherness*. Your natural state is that of pure *being*, fluid and free. You must renounce all other ideas and concepts to reclaim this innate peace, since your life is a dream, and your ultimate goal is to awaken from it.

10. You are Pure Awareness becoming aware of yourself, Divine Consciousness making yourself conscious that you are Consciousness. All things hold the seeds of their past and future and happen on their own, for life unfolds and changes according to the *gunas*, the elements and qualities of nature.

11. Discover That which is permanent in you by developing dispassion for the world, letting go of the ideas that pinch you out of your true essence. Accept things and people as they are, and as they come and go, while relinquishing the need to control anything.

12. You are an expression of the Self, and so is everyone else. What you perceive are concepts arising in your mind. If you are happy, everyone is happy; if you are free, everyone is free; if you are at peace, the world is at peace. The *otherness* you experience as separate is a reflection of your ego; it is unreal, but you can use this reflection to recognize and release the distorted self-perception that makes you suffer.

13. Your essence is eternal; you were never born and you will never die. You are not in the world; the world is in you—or rather, *the world is you*. Be deliberate in your effort to liberate yourself from the root of your unhappiness—the restless, greedy ego-mind that blocks your truth with false identifications and desires leading to discontentment and sorrow.

14. Painful emotions come from false concepts about yourself; they vanish once you see them for what they are—outdated ideas to which you give your power and energy in an attempt to gain validation from your own reflection appearing as *others*. To see this clearly, cultivate a neutral state of *witnessing*, as you allow yourself to be guided from within to express yourself in the world, and surrender to life.

15. Stop believing that you are a doer and see yourself as a vessel of That which manifests everything in perfect synchronicity with everything else. There is no doer; there is only the mysterious *doing* that gets things done, the *unfolding* of Divine Consciousness in infinite shapes and forms. Your suffering ends when you stop deceiving yourself with the idea of being separate, which creates fear, guilt, and the need to control life.

16. Give yourself fully to the present moment to anchor in the fluidity of life itself. Renounce the concept of owning or owing anything, for nothing really belongs to you or is done by you. Everything happens as it is meant to happen, in the Self, for the Self, and by the Self.

17. Let God look after everything. Let life be as it may, choosing to abide in the eternal Presence within that guides you through all experiences, so that you may express who and what you are through your body and mind.

18. Recognize the fleeting nature of sensory desires and experiences, and redirect your attention inward to examine your ego-mind—the I-thought—by seeking its source or concentrating on one thought to exclude all other thoughts, until you reach Pure Silence in your heart, where any sense of individuality blissfully disappears.

19. There are no different selves, only multiple appearances of the one eternal Self. There is no path to the Self; you are the path and the destination. You are never alone, for nothing is separate from you; when your suffering ends, the suffering in the world you are dreaming also ends.

20. Abide as That which is pure Existence, Consciousness, and Bliss (*Sat-Chit-Ananda*), the absolute Reality devoid of all attributes, qualities, and concepts. With the firm, unconditional conviction, "I Am That," remove any sense of limitation or deficiency, and choose to be always happy, refusing any trace of concern, regret, or fear, to dwell in the peace and bliss of the timeless Self you truly are.

* * *

Divine Consciousness will take over your perception once you have matured to the point of not feeling afraid to lose your false identity. If you stay anchored in your heart, in the present, knowing that your reality is produced by the predominant *gunas* in your mind and colored by the past, you can approach any situation with increasing openness and curiosity to see yourself clearly—that is, everything you believe yourself to be.

Accept it all, cultivating self-awareness and humility to witness your life-movie without trying to control it to avoid your responsibilities or your pain. Reflect on the truth that nothing is real but Consciousness, and that all phenomena appear, change, and disappear in Consciousness. It takes time, but eventually this will transform your experience of reality.

Stop seeing obstacles where there are none, for everything you go through is meant to help you remove the self-centeredness that creates suffering. Purify your mind to balance the dense qualities of nature creating attachment, aversion, and fear, so that you may perceive your divinity. Observe your thoughts. Keep turning your attention *from otherness to self*, to know yourself, and from your ego-self to the eternal Self by reflecting on the truth of this divine dream we call life.

Use your body and mind as tools to get to your destination, knowing that you are the destination. Be curious about what lies beyond the appearances while recognizing your mental movie as a reflection that traps you in painful, outdated concepts about yourself. Your Liberation will occur on its own, through Grace, as you remove the shadows blocking your own light, which is the source and backdrop of everything. You will awaken from this cosmic dream when you realize you are the Divine Dreamer, and so is everyone else!

I sincerely hope the Swan Method, as well as the wisdom and tools I have shared with you, will help you uproot the seeds of perception that have prevented you from being at peace. If you have enjoyed the book, I'd greatly appreciate your review where you purchased it (or anywhere it is listed) and spreading the word about it with other spiritual seekers. Make sure to join my mailing list (from any of my websites) for spiritual guidance and inspiration, and to receive notices about courses, workshops, and new books:

YolSwan.com
SoulGuidedCoach.com
YouAreYourHealer.com

Glossary

Advaita Vedanta — Nondualism. A spiritual path of discipline and experience based on the idea that *Brahman* (the Absolute, formless God) is the sole reality and the universe is an illusion (a dream) resulting from the creative power of *Brahman* known as *Maya*.

Ahamkara — The principle of individuality or ego (*I-am-ness*). The original I-thought of the Supreme Self or Cosmic Mind projected onto the human mind.

Antahkarana — The human psyche, or totality of the mind. The "internal instruments" of intellect (*buddhi*), objective mind (*manas*), ego (*ahamkara*), and the field of experience (*chitta*).

Antaratma — The Inner Self or Spirit leading the human mind to the knowledge of the Supreme Self or Supreme Soul.

Asamprajnata Samadhi — Non-cognitive superconsciousness beyond perfect knowledge, where there is no mind field (*chitta*) or thought waves. The Self dwelling in the Self, also known as *nirvikalpa samadhi* and *sahaja samadhi*.

Asana — A series of body postures for health and longevity. The third limb in the yoga system. Also, a seat used exclusively to practice meditation.

Ashtanga Yoga — The path and method for spiritual enlightenment as described by the sage Patanjali in the *Yoga Sutras*. A system of *raja yoga* with eight limbs: *yama, niyama, asana, pranayama, pratyahara, dharana, dhyana,* and *samadhi.*

Atma, Atman — The individual soul as an expression of the *Antaratma, Gyanatma,* and *Paramatma.* The Self.

Bhakti Yoga — The path of devotion through prayer, chanting, mantra, worship, rituals, remembrance of and complete surrender to God.

Bodhisattva — An enlightened being that has put off the highest levels of *nirvana* to help other aspirants attain Liberation. In modern Mahayana Buddhism, a seeker vowing to put others before themselves.

Brahman — The Universal Self or Supreme Reality, the Absolute, formless God. Pure *Being.*

Buddhi — The higher mind or discriminating aspect of the psyche that judges and discerns. The main, subjective screen where Divine Consciousness is projected and cognized.

Chakras — The "wheels" or centers of energy in the energy body connecting the subtle body (mind) to the nervous system and regulating all psycho-physiological aspects and states.

Chitta — The mind field, field of experience, or field of consciousness within the psyche, often simply referred to as *mind.* The equivalent of *buddhi* in Vedanta.

Dharana — Complete concentration on a single object. The sixth limb in the yoga system.

Dharma — The Divine Law of moral duties, virtues, and conduct supporting life. The "path of righteousness" or "right way of living."

Glossary

Dhyan, Dhyana — Meditation, the uninterrupted flow of concentration on a single object until the mind merges with it. The seventh limb in the yoga system.

Gunas — The qualities of nature or cosmic matter evolving from the creative principle of Pure Consciousness or *Brahman*, the Supreme Reality. The energies known as *sattva*, *rajas*, and *tamas* present everywhere, whose constant interplay shapes and maintains the universe—the cosmic dream of the Self.

Gyanatma — The aspect of the Inner Self with complete or perfect knowledge leading to the Supreme Soul or Supreme Self.

Hatha Yoga — The "forceful" practices in the first four limbs of the *ashtanga yoga* system. The traditional system of *asanas* or body postures originally described in the *Matsyenda Samhita*.

Jiva — The individual soul (*atma*) incarnated in a physical body.

Jnana (Gyana) Yoga — The spiritual path of wisdom or Self-knowledge through intellectual understanding, discrimination, and self-inquiry. The merging with Consciousness (or *Brahman*) that dissolves the delusion of duality.

Karma Yoga — The spiritual path of selfless service, of serving God by serving others without expectations or attachment to the outcome of any action. The discipline of *non-action*, or action without ego.

Kundalini Shakti — The feminine spiritual power or principle (a.k.a. *Maya*) that shapes the human body in the womb and eventually guides the incarnated soul (*jiva*) toward Self-realization. The chief prana or vital force from which all other energies arise, along with the ego.

Maha Samadhi — The "Great Liberation" that occurs when the physical body of a fully enlightened saint dies, freeing that soul from *Samsara* and residual karma.

Manas — The lower, objective aspect of the mind that perceives the external world by receiving and recording information through the physical senses. The seat of thinking.

Maya — Illusion. The phenomenological world of appearances hiding the absolute reality of the Self. The principle that makes That which is unmanifest, unchanging, and causeless (the Self or *Brahman*) appear as a multiplicity of attributes and modifications.

Nirvana — In Buddhism, the superconscious state of *no-mind*. The gradual levels of *nirvana* are similar to *samadhi* (or *satori* in Zen), although the term also refers to the state of full enlightenment known as *moksha* or *turiya* in yoga and Advaita Vedanta.

Nyamas — Main spiritual observances: cleanliness, contentment, austerity, study of sacred scriptures, and surrender to God. The second limb in the yoga system.

Paramatma — The Supreme Soul of the Universe. The Supreme Self beyond all manifestation.

Pranayama — Breathing techniques to control the breath to quiet the mind. The fourth limb in the yoga system.

Pratyahara — Withdrawal of the senses to direct the attention away from external objects or stimuli. The fifth limb in the yoga system.

Raja Yoga — The "royal" spiritual path of disciplines and techniques leading to meditation and *samadhi*. Another name for *ashtanga yoga*.

Rajas — One of the three qualities of nature (*gunas*). The energy of activity, movement, passion. The energy that sets in motion all thoughts, desires, and deeds.

Sahaja Samadhi — The original or "natural" non-dual awareness that persists in the waking, sleep, and dream states. A perfect state of Self-realization where the mind has resolved into the Inner Self. Similar to *nirvikalpa* or *asamprajnata samadhi*, as long as no effort is needed to remain in such state.

Samadhi — Perfect or unified consciousness. The superconscious state where the process of concentration, the object of concentration, and the mind become one. There are various stages of *samadhi* to reach complete absorption with the Self until it becomes permanent. The eighth or final limb in the yoga system and the eighth element in the Buddhist path.

Samsara — The cycle of reincarnations. The wheel of deaths and rebirths through which the soul transmigrates according to past karma and unfulfilled desires. The cycle of suffering, or the flow of the mind toward the material world.

Samskaras — Latent impressions from past experiences and actions that become thought waves (*vrittis*) as well as desires and tendencies of perception and behavior (*vasanas*) through which individual life is experienced.

Sasmita Samadhi — Superconscious state accompanied by the knowledge of pure *I-am-ness*. The highest level of *asamprajnata samadhi*, where all mental impressions and tendencies are roasted in Pure Awareness.

Sat-Chit-Ananda (Satchitananda) — "Existence/Truth, Consciousness, and Bliss." The ultimate experience of the unchanging nature of the Supreme Self or God. The source of all reality, the essence and destination of every soul.

Sattva — One of the three qualities of nature (*gunas*). The energy of light, purity, clarity, awareness. The aim of a spiritual seeker is to turn the mind *sattvic* through dispassion, discrimination, and by cultivating virtuous tendencies.

Tamas — One of the three qualities of nature (*gunas*). The energy of darkness, inertia, density, stability, and materiality. It gives the world its three-dimensional density when countered by the light of Consciousness on the mind.

Turiya — The "fourth" state underlying the waking, dreaming, and sleeping states. The original state of Pure Awareness similar to deep, dreamless sleep but with full consciousness.

Vasanas — Desires, motivations, latent impressions. The mental tendencies and habits from past desires and experiences that fuel both the perception and behavior by the agency of ego.

Vipassana — Buddhist insight meditation into the true nature of reality, which is impermanence, dissatisfaction, and suffering.

Vrittis — Thought waves, mental fluctuations, or modifications of the mind. Also, the revolving quality of the mind that churns new thoughts, impressions, desires, and memories from previous thoughts, impressions, desires, and memories.

Yamas — Moral disciplines and restraints: non-violence, truthfulness, non-stealing, sexual continence, and non-hoarding (absence of greed). The first limb in the yoga system.

Yoga — The union with the Divine achieved through the spiritual paths of *bhakti*, *karma*, *raja*, or *jnana yoga*. Both the method and the path, as well as the goal of spirituality. Ultimately, *yoga* is *samadhi*, the superconscious state attained by completely restraining the activity of the mind.

About the Author

YOL SWAN is a spiritual teacher, author, and coach with studies in English literature, music, and clinical homeopathy. Growing up in an intellectual family, she intuitively rejected any and all forms of religion from a very young age; but she perceived life as energy and always felt guided from within.

She awakened to the Divine in her late twenties while spending a few years in almost complete isolation to better understand herself. Then she built a solid spiritual foundation with the personal guidance of enlightened masters from both Buddhist and Hindu traditions, which eventually led her to the path of nondualism or Self-knowledge she now teaches.

With more than thirty years of experience exploring the mind through psychology, spirituality, yoga philosophy, and Advaita Vedanta, she helps people around the world implement the Swan Method to gain emotional and spiritual freedom by comprehending the meaning of their life and the true nature of reality. She lives in Western North Carolina, surrounded by the Blue Ridge Mountains, with the sweetest dog in the world.

You can contact her for speaking engagements through any of her websites or social media:

YolSwan.com
Yol Swan Link Tree: linktr.ee/yolswan

www.ingramcontent.com/pod-product-compliance
Lightning Source LLC
Chambersburg PA
CBHW031411290426
44110CB00011B/339